CH00811085

**“** The world stan
anyone pass w
where he or she is going. **”**

## —William W. Hewitt

D ecide what you want or where you want to be—
then build a bridge to get there! This book shows
you just what steps to take, many of which you may
have never thought of—but which have been proven to
work powerful miracles in the lives of many. Drawing on
his experience as an IBM executive helping people develop to their fullest potential, William Hewitt gets you to
think about yourself and your life in different ways. By
doing so, you will develop the power to enrich your life
beyond your wildest imagination!

This book can make you free in the fullest sense of
the word, rich in the fullest sense of the word, happy in
the fullest sense and successful in the fullest sense. In
other words, you can live the "100% life"! All it takes is
an open mind and some good old-fashioned guts to
embark on an adventure with your higher consciousness. With William Hewitt's expert guidance and humor-
ous, common-sense approach, you will explore your life
purpose, choices, altered states of consciousness, self
hypnosis, meditation, prayer, self-talk, spirituality, astrology, dreams, difficult people, death, and seemingly unrelated topics such as committees, suicide, and good old
boy networks.

Dare to embrace exciting thoughts and ideas never
before considered . . . create a systematic sequence of
events and actions that lead to your goals . . . develop the
character to become the new, real you, with no exceptions . . . build those bridges and set your future in
motion now. Do this—and watch the world step aside to
let you pass on through.

## About the Author

William Hewitt has devoted most of his adult life to training, teaching, motivating, and counseling people. This book is his fifth in a series of self-help, how-to books. He lectures and conducts workshops on personal development, and as a certified hypnotherapist, as well as a professional astrologer, has counseled and guided hundreds of people to capitalize on their strengths, overcome problems, and create better lives for themselves. A former IBM executive and non-commissioned air force officer, he now spends his time writing both for the public and for private industry.

## To Write to the Author

If you wish to contact the author or would like more information about this book, please write to the author in care of Llewellyn Worldwide, and we will forward your request. Both the author and publisher appreciate hearing from you and learning of your enjoyment of this book and how it has helped you. Llewellyn Worldwide cannot guarantee that every letter written to the author can be answered, but all will be forwarded. Please write to:

William W. Hewitt
c/o Llewellyn Worldwide
P.O. Box 64383-323, St. Paul, MN 55164-0383, U.S.A.
Please enclose a self-addressed, stamped envelope for reply, or $1.00 to cover costs. If outside U.S.A., enclose international postal reply coupon.

## Free Catalog from Llewellyn

For more than 90 years Llewellyn has brought its readers knowledge in the fields of metaphysics and human potential. Learn about the newest books in spiritual guidance, natural healing, astrology, occult philosophy and more. Enjoy book reviews, new age articles, a calendar of events, plus current advertised products and services. To get your free copy of the New Times, send your name and address to:

*The Llewellyn New Worlds*
P.O. Box 64383-323, St. Paul, MN 55164-0383, U.S.A.

*Llewellyn's Self-Improvement Series*

# Bridges to Success and Fulfillment

## Techniques to Discover & Release Your Potential

**William W. Hewitt**

Distributed by :
**W. FOULSHAM & CO. LTD.,**
YEOVIL ROAD, SLOUGH, SL1 4JH ENGLAND

FIRST EDITION, 1993

Cover photo © Horticultural Photography, Corvallis, Oregon

Library of Congress Cataloging in Publication Data
Hewitt, William W., 1929–
    Bridges to success and fulfillment : techniques to
discover & release your potential / William W. Hewitt

      p. cm. — (Llewellyn's self-improvement series)
    ISBN 0-87542-323-X : $7.95
    1. Success—Psychological aspects.  I. Title.  II. Series.
BF637.S8H44   1992                       92-35727
1312—dc20                           CIP

Llewellyn Publications
A Division of Llewellyn Worldwide, Ltd.
St. Paul, Minnesota 55164-0383, U.S.A.

## About Llewellyn's Self-Improvement Series

We all desire to live a "full life," one that we can look back on with no regrets. Yet many of us live from day to day feeling that "something" in our life is missing, or that we have become a victim of circumstances which make happiness impossible.

Ironically, even when we desire to make a positive change in our life, we often stick with situations or behaviors that are unhealthy for us, be they bad relationships, unfulfilling work, or addictions to food, money, sex, or drugs.

The greatest barrier to human growth is the illusion of helplessness and powerlessness. It is the illusion that we have no choices in life.

Nothing could be further from the truth. Everyone has inherent resources to succeed if he or she learns to tap into them. And that's where self-empowerment comes in.

To empower yourself means to make choices to improve your life with commitment, style and joyfulness. It is reclaiming your own creative power to change, to love and nurture yourself, and to persevere in obtaining your goals. It is ultimately about creating your own reality.

**Llewellyn's Self-Improvement Series** gives you a direct opportunity to improve yourself and your life through practical, step-by-step guidance from people who have mastered the techniques they share. It challenges you to be the best you can be, to *experience change*, not just read about it. It challenges you to surrender old assumptions and self-deceit in favor of growth and honesty. It challenges you to affect deep and powerful changes in your life.

Congratulations. You have already taken the first, most important step toward reclaiming your own amazing power. You have chosen to read this book. A full and rewarding life is yours for the living.

## Other Books by the Author

*Hypnosis*
*Beyond Hypnosis*
*Tea Leaf Reading*
*Astrology for Beginners*

## Forthcoming

*The Art of Self Talk*

# TABLE OF CONTENTS

# DEDICATION

TO: Jose Silva, who I have never met,
for teaching me more through his work,
research, writing, and classes than I
have learned from any other single source.

TO: Carl L. Weschcke, my friend and
mentor, for giving me a chance.

TO: Dolores, my wife and companion,
for being the wind beneath my wings and
for giving me a wonderful life.

TO:  Leethel Fortney, one of my high
school teachers, for being a loving,
caring person.

TO: Myself for doing the best I can
at any given moment.

# Chapter 1

# Introduction

*Success is to be measured not so much by the position that one has reached in life as by the obstacles which he or she has overcome while trying to succeed.*
Booker T. Washington

Over the years I have been asked hundreds of questions by people who have read my books, articles and stories, heard me lecture, or have counseled with me as either a hypnosis client or an astrology client. Certain subjects and questions have been brought up much more frequently than others, which indicates to me that these are subjects the majority of the general population are concerned about.

This book addresses those subjects which I have been approached on most frequently. I make no attempt to present an exhaustive treatise on each subject. Rather, I offer a brief insight for your edification and consideration.

The contents of this book are based on my meditations, experiences, lectures, books, and letters from readers. Some things I present may make you feel uncomfortable. Some may rub you the wrong way. Some will likely fill voids in your own quest for knowledge and enlightenment.

Some readers may feel offended by some of the subject matter or by my treatment of it. Please do not feel offended because no offense is intended. What is reported here is truth as I have experienced it. If you allow it, the material in this book will enable you to expand your knowledge and awareness. Accept the material in this book as food for thought.

My philosophy embraces the right of all people everywhere to hold their own beliefs as they deem to their benefit. In no way am I intent on altering anyone's belief system. My aim is to offer for consideration what I deeply believe to be truth. You render the final judgement with regard to how my truth fits into your life. Some will find answers in this book that they have long sought. Others may find the contents interesting but not important to them at the present moment. However, they may well find it important at some future moment.

Still others will turn a deaf ear to my words; that certainly is their privilege and right.

I don't ask that you swallow this book "hook, line, and sinker." I do ask that you read with an open, inquiring mind and hold my words in abeyance until you have a chance for your own mind to evaluate my words in relation to you and your state of evolvement. Always, in the final analysis, make up your own mind. Make your own choices, those that make the most sense to you at the moment. Be honest enough with yourself to recognize that the choice you make at one moment may well need to be changed at some future moment when you become more knowledgeable and enlightened.

The sequence of subjects in this book does not imply that one subject is more important than another subject. No one subject is more nor less important than another. All are important.

There is a common thread running through all of these seemingly unrelated subjects. That thread is this: You must evaluate and deal with some aspect of each of the subjects in order for you to progress from where you are at this moment to where you will be tomorrow. By putting the subjects discussed into proper perspective for yourself and then acting on your decisions, you build a bridge from today to tomorrow.

The bridge you build can be strong or it can be rickety and wobbly. The bridge can take you to exactly where you want to be tomorrow, or it can take you to someplace you don't want to be. The kind of bridge you build is determined by your choices, your actions (or inactions), your attitude, the clarity of your thought processes, your decisions—in a word, it depends on *you* alone.

In this book I will show you how to build strong bridges that will take you where you want to go.

This book is part psychology, part philosophy, part how-to methods, part practical common sense, part old fashioned "guts," and part new age esoteric experience for your consideration. Some subjects may strike you as being "off the wall." There is a mix of diversity here, but it is all related to you and the bridges you need to build to tomorrow.

And most importantly, the aim of this book is to motivate you to think for yourself, to open your mind to possibilities that you may not have considered, and to help you become your own person, walking across your own bridge of life, which you deliberately constructed by your own free will and choice.

## Chapter 2

# Tomorrow is Only a Day Away

*I have no yesterdays,*
*Time took them away;*
*Tomorrow may not be*
*But I have Today.*
   Pearl Yeadon McGinnis

Dale Carnegie taught thousands of people through his books and classes to "live in day-tight compartments." Today is all you have to deal with. Enjoy today. Learn today. Solve today's problems. Embrace today enthusiastically with your whole heart and soul. Everyone can handle today.

The great Persian poet Omar Khayyam (1050-1133) taught the same wise lesson poetically:

"Why fret about the unborn tomorrow? Tomorrow has not come. Tomorrow may never come.

"There is only today, and today is ours."

I subscribe wholeheartedly to the wisdom of these two great men, and I recommend you consider doing likewise. Implicit in the teachings of Carnegie and Khayyam is this message: *Take care of today and tomorrow will automatically take care of itself.*

No one has ever achieved happiness and success by doing something tomorrow. Whatever needs to be done must be done today. Then when tomorrow becomes today, do whatever needs to be done today. And so it goes, one day at a time, methodically building an endless chain of happiness, achievement, and success experiences. There is no other way, and because tomorrow is only a day away you don't have to wait long for positive results.

If you want beautiful flowers tomorrow you can't wait until then to plant the seeds, can you? So it is with your life. Success, happiness, and achievement are the flowers of life, and they can be blooming every tomorrow of your life if you plant the seeds today. As each tomorrow becomes a today, that today is filled with the blossoms of happiness, success, and achievement, and you continue to plant more seeds for the next tomorrow's blossoms. This is how life works. There is no mystery to it at all. Just plant some seeds today and they will grow into your blossoms of life.

This book provides you with some seeds to think about and plant today so that you can grow a succession of days that are increasingly happy and worthwhile, in order to have an endless succession of glorious blossoms of life tomorrow.

To be a success, a person really only needs to achieve three basic things:

1. Be responsible for yourself.

2. Interact satisfactorily with society.

3. Make a contribution to society.

Example: A barber earns a living, pays taxes, takes care of business and domestic responsibilities (is a responsible person). The barber charges a fair price, gives good haircuts, and treats customers in a friendly manner and with respect (interacts satisfactorily with society). The barber helps people to be well groomed (makes a contribution to society).

If a person is also fulfilled and happy, then that person is an outstanding success.

There are many aspects to achieving the three basic things described above. There are also many aspects to becoming fulfilled and happy. In reality very little is needed to make a happy life, because you can always find the sun within yourself if you will only search for it.

All you need to do to achieve that outstanding success and to find the sun within is to build bridges from today to tomorrow and then cross them. This book shows you how to build those bridges. As you go through life over a series of self-constructed bridges, you will learn to celebrate life one day at a time.

# Chapter 3

# Duality in Human Beings

*If you have anything really valuable to con-
tribute to the world, it will come through the
expression of your own personality—that
spark of divinity that sets you off and makes
you different from every other living creature.*
Bruce Barton

Each of us is two distinct entities in one: A spiritual entity and a physical entity.

The spiritual is that part of you that is pure, invisi-
ble, intelligence and energy. We will label this as being
your mind.

The physical is that part of you that can be seen,
measured, and weighed. We will label this as being your
body or container.

Your physical part is mortal. Your spiritual part is
immortal.

In this life on earth your physical and spiritual com-
ponents are a team that comprises the totality that is

uniquely you. There is no one else exactly like you.

Your physical body is the vehicle through which your spiritual self expresses and experiences itself in this life.

Through expression and experience, the spiritual has the opportunity to advance and evolve to a higher level of consciousness and awareness.

A simplistic scenario of how our team works is something like this: The mind creates something for the body to do, which the body then does. The result of the body doing its assigned task is that the mind gains valuable feedback from the experience to enable it (the mind) to then create something else for the body to do. It is an endless succession of events like this as long as we are alive—a continuous cycle. Life is a cycle. This mind-body relationship and interaction is the most basic form of bridge-building. I label this as stage one.

Bridge-building becomes more sophisticated when we consciously exercise our willpower to direct our mind to create some specific goal (bridge) that we want. An example might be to become a non-smoker. I label this as stage two.

We advance our bridge-building to even greater sophistication by using techniques and tools such as self-talk, self-hypnosis, meditation, prayer, astrology, or psychic development to direct our mind to create what we want; for example, using your natal astrology chart to help you select an occupation that you are best suited for. I label this as stage three.

We achieve the highest level of sophistication in building bridges when we learn how to allow our higher mind to direct our bridge-building. This stage is usually achieved by years of spiritual bridge-building development through the less sophisticated stages. At this level, the bridge-builder is likely to say something like this, "I love myself and bless myself and release myself to higher mind for guidance." A religious person might express it something like this, "Father, thy will be done with me and through me, and I align my will completely with yours." I label this as stage four.

In this book I will concentrate primarily on the first three stages of bridge-building, because I know you will automatically achieve stage four when you have mastered the three lower stages.

As you do your bridge-building, do not be concerned about stages. Just do whatever works best for you in the specific situation you are dealing with, and everything will work out fine.

My only purpose in discussing the four stages (or levels) of bridge-building is to provide you with more knowledge about how your duality functions as a team, to make you special and to provide you the opportunity to grow to bigger and better achievement and happiness if you choose to do so.

Some of you may have an uncommon problem. The physical aspect of your duality may lack something. Perhaps you are missing an arm or leg. Perhaps your vision is extremely poor, or maybe you are blind, perhaps paralyzed, or you may have a defective heart or some other body part is defective.

This physical debility will not prevent you from functioning as a total person and from building bridges to tomorrow. What it does do is force you to use more of your spiritual nature to compensate for your physical loss.

Helen Keller (1880-1968) was blind and deaf. This certainly is a very serious physical handicap, yet she learned to read (braille), speak, and write. She became an internationally respected author and lecturer—an achievement few achieve. Helen Keller drew on her powerful spiritual nature to overcome tremendous obstacles and achieve greatness. She learned to build bridges to success and happiness in spite of not being able to see or hear.

You, too, can overcome physical problems by calling on your spiritual nature. The power of your spiritual nature is infinite and awesome. This book will provide you with some methods you can use.

True, you may have to redirect your goals. For example, if you have only one leg and you want to be a professional football player you will probably have to scratch that idea in favor of something else you *can* do; perhaps a sportscaster or sports writer, for example.

Today there are a great many one-legged skiers. Who would have thought that possible? There have been one-armed professional baseball players.

Robert Louis Stevenson, the great author of *Treasure Island* and other fine novels, spent most of his adult life bedridden with tuberculosis. The great composer Beethoven was deaf.

Thousands of people have overcome tremendous physical difficulties by drawing on the power of their spiritual nature to build their bridges.

This book is all about using your spiritual nature to build bridges to tomorrow. To show you how to succeed regardless of your physical condition, regardless of your social condition, regardless of anything.

If you can think, you can succeed. This book will show you how to open up your thought processes and use them to your benefit.

From this point on, discard the words "I can't" from your vocabulary and thoughts. Substitute "I can" in your mind and speech.

This is an I CAN book!

# Chapter 4

# Are You a 99% Person?

*Real joy comes not from ease or riches or from the praise of others, but from doing something worthwhile.*

Wilfred T. Grenfell

You've heard, and probably even used, the expression, "It is close enough for government work." The implication, of course, is that "close" is "good enough." You don't need to deliver 100% quality—99% will do just fine.

Think about the 99% attitude for a moment. What if everything in your life was 99% perfect. Would you be happy? Would you think 99% was good enough? After all, only 1% of your life would have glitches. For example, 1% of imperfection would mean things like:

- Your spouse (or lover, fiancé, etc.) would only be unfaithful to you four days a year. Is that acceptable to you?

13

- Your desk dictionary, which has about eighty thousand definitions, would have eight hundred incorrect definitions? Not too bad, huh?

- Your phone, electricity, water, heat, television, and word processor would be out of service due to malfunction about fifteen minutes every day. Minor inconvenience, right?

- Your phone book would have four or more incorrect phone numbers on every page.

- The post office would misdeliver twenty million letters a year. One of those might be a refund check being sent to you or a letter offering you a job.

- You plunk down $20,000 for a new car that is going to be inoperable four days every year. Would you stand for that?

- How long would you live if you stopped breathing for just 1% of the time on just one day—that is 14 minutes?

I think the point is well made: 99% is not good enough!

Take a few moments to think about your occupation. What will 99% performance get you? If you are in the grocery business, which typically has about a 1% net profit margin, you won't make any profit. If you are a writer and your manuscripts are only 99% acceptable, you won't get published. If you are a secretary, 99% performance means you will have three or more typos, spelling errors, and grammatical errors on every page you produce. Do you think you would earn a salary increase?

Think about your leisure time. You are reading a mystery novel and the last 1% of the pages are missing. You never learn the solution to the mystery. You purchase a lotto ticket and it has all but one of the numbers needed to win the million dollars. Close, but you don't win the money.

If you are building a bridge and it falls 1% short of its destination, you will not reach the other side. Or, at best, you would be delayed in reaching the other side while you made repairs and adjustments.

In this book everything is concerned with helping you build a bridge to tomorrow so your tomorrows will be exactly what you want in your life. You will have many bridges to build: goal bridges; health bridges; love bridges; occupational bridges; religious bridges; spiritual bridges; behavior bridges; lifestyle bridges; and on and on.

And you must build each bridge with 100% devotion, effort, faith, determination, persistence, clarity of thought, responsibility, and belief in your right to achieve what you want.

If you build your bridge with anything less than 100% of everything you have to offer, you will achieve less than 100% of the results you want. If your bridge is only a little bit short, you can patch it up with more effort and time. If your bridge doesn't even get you close to where you want to be, you will need to reevaluate what you want and where you need to do a better job (a 100% job). Then begin to build a new bridge.

To be a successful bridge-builder, start right now to develop a 100% attitude. Say to yourself, "I give one hundred percent to everything I do. I do not take a half-hearted approach to anything, because I do not settle for less than one hundred percent success."

In the morning when you go to the bathroom, look into the mirror and remind yourself that you have a 100% attitude about life. Look yourself straight into your eyes and say out loud, "I am a one hundred percent person. I am a winner in life and that is the way I like it."

Throughout the day remind yourself that you have a 100% attitude. Do it mentally or out loud as you wish. Do it in the car when you are driving. Do it while working. The important thing is to constantly remind yourself of this commitment to yourself. After a short while you will have programmed yourself to have a 100% success attitude about everything you do.

Great athletes have a 100% attitude about their sport; great musicians, about their music; great thespians, about their acting. But look how often you read in magazines and newspapers where these people have personal lives that are in a shambles. Why is that?

It is because they have built only one bridge—a bridge to only their sport, to their music, or to their acting. They did not build bridges to the rest of their tomorrows in the other aspects of their life. They took a one dimensional approach to life.

There is no need to be one dimensional in your outlook on life. You are multi-dimensional, and you are capable of having success and happiness in every aspect of your life. When you start building your bridges to tomorrow, don't hold back. Cover all the bases you want. Make whatever attitude adjustments you need to, set your sights on all the goals you really want, and then set about making it happen.

One caution: Be sure you really want something before you build the bridge to get it. The reason is that you will get whatever you build a bridge to, and when you cross that bridge you may discover that you don't want what is on the other side tomorrow. Of course, you can usually undo things by dismantling that bridge, crossing back over the other way, or by building a new bridge. But believe me, it is far more difficult to undo something than it is to do it right in the first place.

Let me give you an example of what I am talking about in the preceding paragraph. The most common example I have encountered of someone building a bridge they regret is this: A woman sets her mind to marry a certain man, and she goes all out 100% to get him. She builds her love bridge, crosses over it, and marries the man. The man is an alcoholic and is abusive; the signs were readily apparent before she built the bridge. But she ignored the truth, glossed over the signs, made excuses for his behavior. She wanted him because he was so handsome and was the life of the party. He liked to have a good time. He was good in bed. He was the high school jock, a star athlete. She would be the envy of all the girls when she got him for her own. Besides, she reasoned, she could change him after they were married.

Wrong! She crossed over her self-made love bridge into a life of living hell.

If she had built a bridge to greater awareness first, she wouldn't have even wanted to build a bridge of love to that particular man. She would have had better sense.

To try to undo the nightmare of a bad marriage is a nightmare in itself. Divorce, which is often nasty, is always draining, emotionally and financially. There are custody battles if there are children, which often cause emotional damage to those children. And in some cases there is violence where the man (usually) physically harms his wife. Undoing a bad bridge to tomorrow is always difficult and is often an ordeal.

This scenario illustrates several points:

1. If you become a 100% person, you will get what you want, even if it isn't beneficial for you.

2. You need to exercise good judgment before you build the bridge.

3. You need to set your priorities when building bridges. The place to start is with yourself. Put yourself in balance. Adjust your attitude for success in only those things that are beneficial for you. Establish your own emotional maturity before you pursue a goal in an immature manner.

4. If you build a bridge to the wrong place, it is usually difficult to undo it. It is better to use your good sense beforehand and build a good bridge to where you really are sure you want to be.

First prepare yourself mentally, spiritually, physically, and emotionally to be a responsible citizen of the universe. Then go after those external goals. You will then have a 100% successful life.

I lay the following cornerstone at the beginning of every bridge I start: "I want to achieve this goal with harm to no one." That way there is no way I can complete the bridge unless it is beneficial to me and will not harm anyone else.

Because of this, there have been a number of bridges I started that I never completed. And 100% of the bridges I did complete have brought me great happiness and success.

I suggest you lay a similar cornerstone for all your bridges.

The sequence for building bridges to your tomorrow should be this:

1. Adjust your attitude and behavior to be a 100% person.

2. Lay your "harm to no one" cornerstone.

3. Build your personal bridges to prepare yourself in every respect to be a responsible citizen of the universe.

4. Build your external bridges for all those goals and achievements you want for all your tomorrows.

## GO FOR IT WITH ZEST!

If you should build a bridge that takes you to where you do not want to be (i.e., bad marriage, wrong job, etc.), then work with a 100% effort to dismantle that bridge and replace it with a good bridge.

Do not ever resign yourself to live with the results of a defective bridge. To do so is to limit your life, happiness, and success. Do not settle for anything less than 100% good solid bridges to where you want to be.

I am confident that 99% of you reading this book will strive to be 100%. I wish I could be confident that 100% of you will.

# Chapter 5

# Get Out of the Rain!

*The question is not what a person can scorn,*
*or disparage, or find fault with, but what he or*
*she can love, and value, and appreciate.*
                                              John Ruskin

There are two basic kinds of people in the world: Rain people and Sun people.

A rain person goes through life with a dark cloud overhead. Life is dismal and dreary. They are always being rained on by life's circumstances. Like being in the rain, they are uncomfortable and are always getting splashed by people passing them. They want to get out of the rain but don't know how. Many don't even know how to get an umbrella of courage to buffer them from the onslaught of life's rain. So they plod on aimlessly with no plan of action, hoping that somehow things will work out. Most often they are losers in life.

A sun person goes through life in blazing sunlight. If there are any clouds at all they are small, white, puffy ones. Life is cheery and bright. They are warm and comfortable. Their path is well lighted so they can see where they are going and what their options are. Because of this, they know things will work out just fine for them. Most often they are winners in life.

The principal difference between a rain person and a sun person is *attitude*. Attitude is vitally important when it comes to building your bridges to tomorrow. A rain person is more likely to build a defective bridge or a bridge to the wrong destination. A sun person is more likely to build a strong bridge to the right destination.

In the balance of this chapter I am going to depict the profiles of a rain person and a sun person. Make note of each rain person trait you have, because it will be to your advantage to make an attitude adjustment with regard to that trait so that it is changed to a sun person trait. Very few people are 100% rain people or sun people. We all tend to be a blend of both. As long as we are predominantly sun people, we are in good shape. What we need to do is identify our rain person traits and then eliminate them, substituting a sun person trait in its place. The better job we do of this, the better equipped we are to build strong, successful bridges, and thus obtain the maximum joy and achievement we can in life.

Let me begin by telling you a true story from history about a profound sun person, Leonidas, who was the Spartan king from 490–480 B.C.

Leonidas was in his tent making battle plans for his 200-man army against an invading 2,000-man army. One of his officers rushed into the tent and breathlessly expressed his concern about the ten to one odds against them. "Sir," the officer said, "the enemy's arrows are so thick against the sky that they blot out the sun."

"Good," Leonidas answered, "I do my best work in the shade."

Then Leonidas led his troops in a counterattack and defeated the invading army.

That kind of gutsiness makes you a winner in life. Leonidas knew he was a winner. He never doubted it for a moment. He knew where he was going.

The world stands aside to let anyone pass who knows where he/she is going. Keep this in mind when you build your bridges to tomorrow.

Now let's examine profiles of rain people and sun people.

## *Rain People*

- Basic philosophy: Life is a manure sandwich, which must be distastefully choked down against your will.

- Things happen *to* them.

- Elderly rain people: It is too late to change or to achieve now. The only major thing they have to look forward to is their own funeral. They frequently scan the obituaries for funerals to attend; I call this the funeral syndrome.

- Key phrase is I CAN'T!

- Are not in control of their own life. Other people, life's circumstances, the government, etc. control their life.

- Create a self-fulfilling prophecy of defeatism and doom.

- Experience little or no real joy in life. The closest they come is an occasional chuckle at a TV sitcom.

- Are usually intimidated easily.

- Most often get the short end of business deals.

- Think that life is to be endured, not enjoyed. Joy and reward come only after death. It is a struggle to try to keep from sliding backwards, and death is the only relief to look forward to. (Unfortunately, some religious sects promote a negative way of life: Suffer now and rejoice after death.) If you happen to be in this situation, you may want to think about switching to a sect that is more supportive of your beliefs.

- Rarely are successful to any significant degree.

- Generally are apathetic. Rarely vote, rationalizing, "What difference does it make?"

- Talk more about their troubles; gripe; gossip. Rarely talk about ideas and achievement.

- Are afraid to take the risk of becoming a sun person.

- See the difficulty in every opportunity.

## *Sun People*

- Basic philosophy: Life is a tender, juicy steak sandwich to be eaten with joy, savoring each succulent bite willingly.

- Make things happen the way they want them to be.

- Elderly sun people: It is never too late to change or to achieve. Life has been great, and will continue to be great. Funerals are for dead people, and I am not dead yet.

- Key phrase is I CAN!

- Are in control of their own life. They do not allow circumstances to control them. They control the circumstances.

- Create a self-fulfilling prophecy of winning and success.

- Experience the greatest joys they can squeeze out of life. They find joy everywhere.

- Are rarely ever intimidated.

- Most often get a fair shake in a business deal because they are not willing to settle for less than a fair deal.

- Think that life is to be enjoyed and that rewards can be gotten now through living a full life. Life is not a struggle; it requires work and determination, but one can keep moving forward. Joy and reward will come after death also. Death will come when it will come—in the meantime, live life to the fullest.

• Usually are successful to some degree.

• Rarely are apathetic. They vote because they know they do make a difference. To quote *Stubborn Ounces* by Bonaro W. Overstreet: "You say the little efforts that I make will do no good: they never will prevail to tip the hovering scale where Justice hangs in balance. I don't think I ever thought they would. But I am prejudiced beyond debate in favor of my right to choose which side shall feel the stubborn ounces of my weight."

• Talk about ideas and achievement. Rarely gripe, gossip, or talk about their problems.

• Realize that the biggest risk in life is to do nothing, and they are not guilty of that.

• See the opportunity in every difficulty.

## A Few Examples

**Example #1:** You order a dinner in a restaurant. The salad is inedible—the lettuce is wilted with brown edges and the cucumbers are soggy and shriveled. The rest of the meal is okay.

A rain person may or may not eat the salad and would keep his/her mouth shut, rationalizing that the baked potato was quite good, so why complain.

A sun person would not eat the salad and would politely ask the waitress to do something about it—either a satisfactory salad or have the salad's cost deducted from the bill. If the waitress couldn't, or wouldn't, make an adjustment, the sun person would speak to the manager; not ranting and raving, but politely and firmly insisting on restitution.

**Example #2:** You give an automobile dealer a $100 deposit for a specific car, which he will get ready for you to pick up tomorrow. You return and find that the special wire wheel covers you requested are not on the car. The dealer says he can't give you the wheel covers for the previously agreed on price. He now wants $400 more. You say no deal, and ask for your deposit back. The dealer refuses, saying you made a deal for this car, which you must honor or else lose your deposit.

A rain person would either shell out an additional $400, or else would walk away and lose the $100 deposit, rationalizing, "Well, I guess I learned a lesson from this."

A sun person would not give up, going to the president of the corporation, to the Better Business Bureau, or whatever until he/she got the deposit refunded.

**Example #3:** You book a package tour through a travel agent for specific lodging and amenities in a foreign country. When you arrive, the first class hotel you paid for has no reservation for you. It seems they are off-loading their overbookings to a dirty, cheap hotel with no amenities. The food at the cheap hotel is deplorable and the meals that were supposed to come with the lodging are unfit for consumption, forcing you to spend more money in some better restaurants. You make numerous phone calls back to the travel agency in the United States, but are always told that no one with authority is in the office. You ask them to return your phone calls, but they don't. A countryside guided tour that you had paid for doesn't even exist; the locals tell you that the tour was discontinued over a year ago. What do you do when you return to the United States?

A rain person would probably figure, "That's life" and do nothing. A more gutsy rain person might tell the travel agent what happened, hoping to get a partial refund. When the travel agent refused to give a refund, the rain person would meekly accept his/her fate and forget it.

A sun person would put the entire episode in writing with supporting documentation and present it to the head of the travel agency and request a specific dollar amount of refund. If the travel agency refused, the sun person would raise forty kinds of hell until he/she got the refund no matter how long it took.

The preceding three examples are not made up. Each of these happened to me personally, and I handled each one as a sun person and got what I wanted. Here is a brief reconstruction:

In Example #1, I showed the waitress the salad. She said, "Sorry," but made no attempt to make it right. I talked to the manager and was given a refund.

In Example #2, I wrote a letter immediately to Lee Iacocca, furnishing the complete details. Less than a week later the General Manager of the car agency phoned to apologize and he immediately sent me a $100 check refund on my deposit.

In Example #3, the travel agency said, "Tough! That is the chance you take when you go to a foreign country." They refused to refund a penny. I went to the Better Business Bureau with my case. The BBB hammered on the travel agency, and I ended up getting a larger refund than I originally requested.

There is a message here, folks. It pays to be a sun person. Let me make one thing clear—sun people are not troublemakers. They just refuse to be intimidated, and they stand up for their rights. If that causes problems for others, it is because the others were trying to usurp the sun person's rights; therefore, they (the others) deserve to have problems.

Think about this example from history: King George III of England viewed Patrick Henry as being a trouble-maker. We view Patrick Henry as being a hero and a patriot. King George was the problem, not Patrick Henry. Patrick Henry was a sun person, and he refused to be intimidated. King George deserved all the grief the thirteen colonies gave him during our Revolutionary War.

## Summary

The profiles of the rain and sun people give you a good idea of what bridges you need to build to become a sun person and which ones you need to tear down if you have some rain person traits. Now it is merely up to you to make your choices and get busy on your bridges.

I would like to leave you with a story that relates to the elderly rain person trait of believing "it is too late to change or to achieve."

A ten year old boy was in a store purchasing candy. He said to the storekeeper, "I'll bet you really like working here, don't you?"

The storekeeper frowned and said, "I hate it! The only reason I am here is that I inherited this store when I was twenty years old when my father died. I really wanted to be an accountant."

"Then why don't you sell the store and go to school to be an accountant now?" the boy asked.

"What? Make a change now? I am going to be fifty years old next year!"

"Won't you still be fifty years old next year whether you become an accountant or stay in this store?"

The boy's wisdom is profound. If you are alive, it is never too late. Remember, Colonel Harlan Sanders started with nothing except guts and a recipe for preparing fried chicken when he was sixty-six years old, and he went on to create the Kentucky Fried Chicken® empire.

Think about it, then make *your* move. Of course, you don't have to make an attitude adjustment if you don't want to.

A rain person doesn't *always* lose, and a sun person doesn't *always* win—but that is the way to bet on it!

# Chapter 6

# **Choices**

*Ideals are like stars. You will not succeed in touching them with your hands; but like the seafaring man, you choose them as your guides, and, following them, you will reach your destiny.*

Carl Schury

Examine your life critically and objectively. Strip away all the window dressing, gingerbread, and foliage. Toss aside superficial things like physical appearance, education, family name, and other people's opinions. Throw away blame. Put all your excuses in the trash can.

When you finish stripping away the peripheral things that hang on to you and mask you, you end up with the one thing that really is you. You are a pure, intelligent energy that does only one thing in this life . . . you make choices.

That is what life is all about. Making choices. Your life might be diagramed simplistically like the chart on the following page.

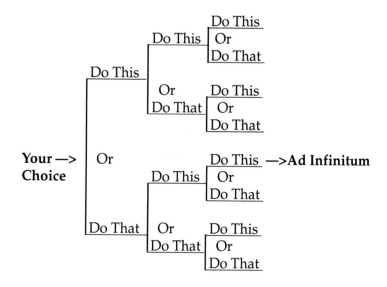

The chart shows that you are faced with a choice. Depending on your choice, you embark on a certain path of experience that presents other choices. Depending on those choices, you embark on still other paths with other choices. And so on. It never ends. You can always choose and go on, but you can never go back and completely undo a choice you have already made.

The implications of this are awesome. It means that at any given moment in your life, you are where you are, doing what you are doing, as a direct result of all the choices you have made in your life up to that moment. Simply put, it means that you and you alone are totally responsible for you. No one else is responsible. Just you.

Of all the people you will meet in your lifetime, you are the only one you will never leave nor lose. To the problems of your life, you are the only solution. To the questions of your life, you are the only answer. In short: You are responsible for you and for your choices.

"My father forced me to be an engineer," you plead. "I wanted to be an accountant."

"Baloney!" I reply. "Your father presented a strong influence on you to be an engineer, but you chose to allow his influence to dominate you. Don't pass the buck. It was your choice. You could have refused to give in to his influence and have done something else."

And so it is with all, whether it be a parent, a peer, the government, or whatever. You have the choice. Of course, there are times when it is prudent to choose to be influenced. For example, the government presents a strong influence to pay your taxes. If you choose not to pay, the path you then present to yourself might lead you to jail. But the choice is always yours.

More often than not, our bad choices are those we make as a result of allowing someone else to influence our decisions. Bad choices can often be undone or corrected, usually after much grief and building new bridges, but they cannot always be corrected. Here is a story to illustrate the point.

A man was walking along a path in the woods one cold, windy day when he heard a voice call from a bush next to the path.

"Please help me," the voice called. "I am freezing to death."

The man looked toward the bush and saw a rattlesnake lying on the ground, shivering. Being cold blooded, the rattlesnake needed warmth or it would die.

"But you are a deadly rattlesnake," the man said. "It would be dangerous for me to help you."

"Please," the snake pleaded. "I will die without

your help. If you just put me inside your clothing next to your body I can get warm and live. I promise I will not bite you if you help me."

"You promise?"

"Yes, I promise." the snake confirmed. "I will not bite you."

So the man, feeling sorry for the rattlesnake, pushed his apprehension aside and picked it up and tucked it inside his shirt so the snake could get warm and live.

The man continued his walk, and soon the snake warmed up and was fine.

Then the man felt a pain in his side as the snake sank its fangs into him.

"You bit me!" the man cried. "You promised you wouldn't do that. Now I will die!"

"Don't blame me," the snake answered. "It is your fault. You knew what I was when you picked me up."

Keep this story in mind whenever you are in a situation where someone is trying to influence your choices in a direction you really don't want to go. The person who influences you doesn't have to live with your choices. Only you live (or die in some cases) by your choices. Wouldn't you rather call your own shots instead of letting someone else call them for you?

The ability to choose is a powerful tool that you can use to create the kind of life you wish for yourself. All of your bridges to tomorrow are built with your choices.

If you are an alcoholic and want to change, you can choose to do so. You can seek help. You can program your mind to stop drinking. There are a number of options open to you, if you choose to exercise them.

And so it is with any aspect of your life. You can

decide in your mind what you really want, and then you can make it happen.

There are many excellent books on the market to help you. There are people and agencies that can help. And most importantly, there is an infinite amount of self-help buried deep within yourself that you can tap. All the wonders you seek are within yourself.

The important things to glean from this short chapter are:

1. You always have choices.

2. You are totally responsible for your choices.

3. You can learn to exercise better choices and thus create whatever kind of life you wish.

4. You cannot erase a choice once it is made. As the poet Omar Khayyam wrote eight centuries ago: "The Moving Finger writes; and, having writ, moves on: nor all your piety nor wit shall lure it back to cancel half a line, nor all your tears wash out a word of it."

5. You can sometimes, but not always, reduce or eliminate the results of poor choices by initiating new, good choices. In other words, life is like a suit of clothes, and you are the tailor. You can choose to make whatever kind of suit you want; one that fits well, or one that fits poorly; one made of good quality fabric, or one of inferior fabric; one well stitched, or one full of holes. Perfect or tattered.

Start today to be more aware of your choices. Exercise your choices the way you really want . . . not as someone else thinks is best for you. Become a whole person as you wish . . . the real you as you perceive yourself.

Tailor your life to fit well, be of top quality fabric, with no holes, and beautiful throughout.

You can do it if you so choose. The choice is yours alone. Start now to build your bridges by using strong, sound choices as the construction material.

Henry Ward Beecher wrote, "God asks no man whether he will accept life. That is not the choice. You must take it. The only choice is how."

# Chapter 7

# Rights, Responsibility, and Karma

*We live in deeds, not years; in thoughts,*
  *not breaths;*
*In feelings, not in figures on a dial.*
*We should count time by heart-throbs.*
*He most lives who thinks most, feels the*
  *noblest, acts the best.*

Philip James Bailey

You have probably heard the adage, "Your right to swing your arm ends where my nose begins."

That adage pretty well sums up what an individual's rights are. You have the right to think, say, and do anything you want with only one proviso: You do not have the right to infringe on, usurp, or violate the rights of another person. That gives us all nearly unlimited freedom, does it not?

Unfortunately, violation of rights runs rampant throughout the world. This is because human beings have the uncanny ability to rationalize their unjustifiable actions as being within their rights. Of course, that is fallacious thinking.

Governments do not have the right to suppress or usurp the rights of any of its law abiding citizens, even though they do so under a smoke screen of double talk, rhetoric, and warped rationalization.

Government agencies do not have the right to release dangerous criminals back into society, even though they do so under various rationalized guises such as rehabilitation, or the cells are too crowded, or there weren't enough television sets for every prisoner, or whatever.

Perpetrators of crimes have no right to commit crimes, even though some elements of society excuse them because the criminal says he was spanked for bed wetting when he was fourteen years old, and it left him unable to tell right from wrong.

You do not have the right to lie about someone, even though you rationalize that the person is not a good person and deserves it.

If you are a disease carrier, you do not have the right to take deliberate actions that cause you to spread the disease. In fact, you have an inherent responsibility to do everything in your power to not spread the disease.

I think you get the picture. You can fill in the rest of the extremely long list.

You do have the right to happiness, freedom, peace, equality under the law, et cetera. You have the right to defend and protect your rights.

Whenever anyone or any organization takes an action to violate your rights, you have the right to take appropriate action to stop that violation. The moment someone violates your rights, he/she automatically forfeits his/her rights in that matter. You have the right to stop him/her—the right to defend yourself.

The government grossly violated, or tolerated the violation of, the rights of black people for nearly two centuries. Martin Luther King and many others fought to stop those violations. They had every right to do so. And they fought back without violating the rights of others. This is a beautiful lesson for all of us.

What Reverend King realized was that Rights is a two-sided coin. The flip side of that coin is Responsibility.

You have the right to build all the bridges to tomorrow that you want to. However, it is incumbent on you to also exercise responsibility when you do it. Rights and responsibility must be inseparable, otherwise chaos, injustice, and failure will surely follow.

Let me give you an example from United States history where rights and responsibility were not exercised together, to illustrate my point.

During World War II, President Franklin Delano Roosevelt ordered the incarceration of all American citizens of Japanese blood. These were law-abiding, loyal, tax-paying, valuable American citizens, and the government took their property and money and locked them up as though they were common criminals. Common criminals are always given a fair trial in the United States. These were innocent men, women, and children—yet they were given no hearing of any kind. In the interests of national security, they were deprived of their civil rights. Mr. Roosevelt had stretched his authority as President to the breaking point.

Nearly fifty years passed before the government acknowledged, almost half-heartedly, that a grievous error had been made. They promised to make a token restitution. As I write this, that restitution has not been made, and I personally doubt that it will be. How can you correct that magnitude of wrong?

There is one other serious damage resulting from this irresponsible act. The Presidency itself lost faith with the American people, and citizens no longer trust their government the way they used to. Will this ever be repaired? I don't know. Perhaps in time, but I think not in my lifetime, nor in the generation following.

I recount this true act of irresponsibility to make you aware of the serious consequences that can result when you do not exercise your rights in a responsible way.

The ancient Chinese taught: To not take action before foreseeing the outcome of your action, and to approach the realization of your goals with caution. These are wise words indeed. Heed them when you build and cross your bridges.

Suppose you want to build a bridge to wealth. You decide to go into a business that you foresee as giving you the means of obtaining that wealth. If you build integrity and honesty into that bridge, you will obtain that wealth, and rightly so, because you have displayed responsibility in your actions.

But suppose you see a way to get even more wealth by cheating in the way you conduct your business; perhaps by lying about the extent of your income on your tax return, or perhaps by selling inferior merchandise. Whatever. You put a building block of dishonesty into your bridge. You are now acting in an irresponsible manner. Trouble will follow as a result. You created negative karma, and it must be balanced out; that is universal law.

Let's talk about karma to see what it is and how it fits in with your bridge-building.

Each of us is an energy field. By our actions we cause our energy field to be either positive (good in the karmic sense) or negative (bad in the karmic sense).

Whenever we exercise our rights in a responsible way, we create a positive (good) karma.

Whenever we violate the rights of others or behave in an irresponsible way, we create negative (bad) karma.

The karma we create is ours; we own it, and by universal law we must deal with it.

In order for us to evolve in our journey through eternity, we must have more positive karma than negative. The ultimate goal is to achieve 100% positive karma. If we possess more negative karma than positive, we regress and lose what we have previously gained. If we have equal amounts of negative and positive karma; we do not evolve to a higher level nor do we slip backward; we are sort of in limbo.

Universal law says that eventually all negative karma must be cancelled out by positive karma for each and every one of us. Sometimes that cancellation takes place right away or later in this same lifetime. Sometimes that cancellation takes place in a subsequent lifetime. In our current lifetime, most of us are probably cancelling out some negative karma we created in a previous lifetime.

Here is an example of what might be immediate negative karma cancellation. You are a physician who gained much of your wealth by illegally selling drug prescriptions to drug addicts. You get caught. You lose your medical license and reputation. You lose all your wealth and property due to legal fees and fines. You are sent to prison. Your family is left destitute and heartbroken. You live a long time in prison, where memories of your actions haunt you every day. When you eventually get out of prison, you are old. Your health is broken. No one, including your family, will have anything to do with you. You become a skid-row bum and die as an alcoholic, alone in an alley.

I think you get the picture. When you build your bridges, do so with responsibility and without violating the rights of others. That way you will succeed and you will collect positive karma in the process.

### *Summary*

In your bridge-building, you must exercise your rights in a responsible way in order to construct good bridges.

If you do not act in a responsible way, you set the stage for chaos and failure.

If you do not respect the rights of others, you set the stage for failure and you collect negative karma for yourself, which you must deal with at some point.

Karma is the yardstick by which your worth as a human being is measured. The whole concept of living is to collect positive karma, not negative karma, thereby enhancing your worthiness and ensuring your success and happiness.

When you build your bridges, make sure you exercise responsibility, exercise your rights without violating the rights of someone else, and then you will have ensured that your tomorrow will be exactly what it should be and what you want it to be.

## Chapter 8

# If You Want Chicken, You Must First Have an Egg

*The eagle was once nothing but an egg, but what would we know about the nature, the meaning, the possibilities of that egg had we never seen the eagle soaring in splendor against the sky?*

Author Unknown

If a chicken egg is fertilized and incubated, it eventually gives birth to a chicken. The egg has become a universal symbol of new ideas, new starts, and creativity. The chicken is symbolic of the goal attained, i.e., the birth as a result of the idea, creativity, and so forth.

In the Great Depression of the 1930s, having chicken every Sunday for dinner was symbolic of some semblance of prosperity in those bleak times. Sunday chicken dinner was a goal that said, "We are doing okay." In a sense, the chicken dinner was a bridge people built to keep their hopes up at a time when things seemed hopeless.

This chapter is going to examine the building of chicken bridges. First you must have an egg.

For example, one of my chicken bridges is the writing and publication of this book. For the book to be created, I had to have an egg. The egg was the concept I used of showing the relationship among seemingly unrelated subjects in such a way as to guide people to a better way of life.

First I fertilized the egg by brainstorming my mind for subjects at random, such as: dreams, chickens, hypnosis, astrology, self talk, choices, greed, religion, spirituality, compromise, success, failure, goal setting, occupations, death, committees, karma, rights, responsibility, stories of famous people, and on and on. I ended up with a list of around a hundred items.

Then I let the idea and the list turn over and over in my mind for several weeks. I talked out loud to myself about it. I wrote a few sketchy notes as ideas popped into my mind. I was incubating my egg.

Soon the common thread running through all those subjects became clear in my mind. I saw how they all related to building bridges to tomorrow. I started to write, and slowly the egg began to crack as I wrote more and more. When I finished, the egg broke all the way open, and my chicken (this book) was born.

Thomas Alva Edison wanted a chicken of light. He wanted to illuminate the whole world. His egg was the concept that he could apply electricity to some sort of filament in a vacuum inside a glass container and cause light to be created.

Edison incubated his idea through over 9,000 experiments while trying to find a filament that would create the light he sought. He had completed over 8,000 experiments when someone tried to destroy his egg. That person said, "Mr. Edison, why don't you give up? Your dream is impossible. You have failed over 8,000 times!"

Edison replied, "I have not failed at all. I have discovered over 8,000 things that won't work for my purposes. That means I am now close to discovering the one that will work."

Edison persisted. One day, after over 9,000 experiments, he made a filament from tungsten, a hard, brittle, corrosion resistant element extracted from wolframite, scheelite, and other minerals, having the highest melting point and lowest vapor pressure of any metal. When Edison applied electricity to the tungsten in a vacuum in a glass container, the tungsten glowed brilliantly and kept on glowing hour after hour, giving off beautiful light. Edison's chicken, the electric light bulb, had been born, or hatched. As a result, the entire world is lighted.

There is a lesson here for all of us. We need to emulate Edison's positive attitude and irrepressible determination if we want our eggs (ideas) to hatch and give birth to our chickens (goals).

Let's look at a few more egg/chicken stories that furnish some additional perspectives.

The late Nat King Cole was a piano player. His dream was to earn a living as a piano player, because that was what he loved to do. He was happy playing in night clubs. He figured he already had his chicken.

One night he was playing "Sweet Lorraine" when a big spending drunk insisted that Nat sing the song. Nat smiled and said, "I am not a singer. I just play piano."

The drunk complained to the manager, who then ordered Nat to sing "Sweet Lorraine" or else he would be fired.

So Nat Cole sang. And when he started to sing in his perfectly toned, soft, beautiful voice, all the noise in the club stopped. Everyone listened. The rest is history. Nat King Cole went on to become one of the greatest balladeers in music history. Nat had given birth to more chicken than he ever dreamed existed.

What happened to Nat King Cole is called serendipity. The dictionary defines serendipity as "the faculty of making fortunate and unexpected discoveries by accident." In common usage, it means that while you are in the process of trying to achieve something, you encounter an unexpected turn of events that causes you to achieve something better, greater, and more fortunate than you were looking for in the first place.

Nat Cole set out to be a pianist in a nightclub, and, because of an unexpected request from a drunk, he became a world-renowned singer.

Christopher Columbus set out to find a new route to India, and unexpectedly discovered America. Serendipity again.

Jose Silva, an American of Mexican heritage, lived in Laredo, Texas, where he fathered a large family. His children are all successful adults now, but in their younger years in school they had a problem. The problem was that their grades in school consistently were lower than the grades of Caucasian children.

Silva was certain that his children were intelligent, in spite of mediocre or poor school grades. Was racial prejudice the problem? He allowed that prejudice might be a factor, but he was certain that there was more to it than that. His "egg" was to solve the problem of his children's poor grades.

He trained himself in hypnosis and then used hypnosis on his children. He gave them hypnotic suggestions that they had superior intelligence; that they were equal to any other person regardless of race, religion, or creed; that they would have superb memories; that they would love school and love to learn, and so forth.

The results were dramatic and immediate. His children quickly zoomed to the top of their classes. Ultimately, several of them tested out at the genius level.

It would seem that Silva's chicken had been hatched because he had solved the problem of his children's school grades. But this is only the beginning of the story. There were a great many more chickens to be born, so to speak.

While Silva worked with his children and hypnosis, he developed an insatiable desire to know what the mind was, how it worked, and what its limits were, if indeed it had any limits.

Silva studied and experimented relentlessly over a period of years, during which he became an expert in the mind and its usage. From this he developed what may well be the greatest training program to date for using the mind. Silva Mind Control International is a mental training program that goes well beyond hypnosis, and gives phenomenal results instantly. I am a graduate of Silva's basic training and graduate training, and can attest to the validity and value of Jose Silva's work.

Silva's chicken pot runneth over, so to speak.

I set out with two buddies in January, 1951, to attend a lecture that unexpectedly was a bore, so we left.

So that the trip to New Orleans wouldn't be a waste, my buddies decided to go on The President, a paddle-wheel nightclub boat that cruised the Mississippi River, so they could dance. I don't dance, but had to go along because it wasn't my automobile.

On the boat I met Dolores Quey, who was to become my wife. It was one of the most fortunate events of my life, and we have been happily married for over forty years as I write this. Serendipity!

As you build your bridges and cross them, keep your senses alert for serendipitous events that can unexpectedly bring you more chicken than you ever anticipated.

Identify your egg and the chicken you want to be born from it, then build your bridge and go after the chicken with your whole heart, energy, and determination. And every once in a while serendipity will join you on your bridge, and you will hit the jackpot, or should I say "chicken pot."

# Chapter 9

# The Highest Calling

*The poor person is not he or she who is*
   *without a cent,*
*But he or she who is without a dream.*

Harry Kemp

Much of my astrological and hypnotherapy counseling over the years has dealt with helping people select the best occupational path to follow. Whether I am using a natal astrology chart to define someone's strengths and weaknesses or using hypnosis to help someone define and set goals, the question I am invariably asked is, "What should I do with my life?" or "What job is best for me?"

The answer to those questions lies within the one asking, not within me. I am merely skilled at helping people dig out their own answers from deep within themselves.

Experience has shown me one very important fact: All jobs are important. No honest job is demeaning or shameful. No job is more dignified or prestigious than another. Dignity and prestige are qualities that reside within a person, not within an occupation.

There are always people who try to put other people down. It is a weakness they have within themselves that they refuse to accept. The executive who looks down on the man who empties trash cans is displaying inferior behavior. The school superintendent who thinks he/she is superior to the teachers under his/her authority is displaying inferior behavior. The hotel manager who treats the maids as though they were subservient, inferior people is behaving in an inferior manner. And so forth.

Superior behavior is that behavior displayed by any person in any job with competence, integrity, caring, and honesty. Superior behavior in any job is never displayed by an attitude of being more worthy than someone in some other job.

Whether you are providing a service or a product, whether you are in the public eye or behind the scenes, whether you attend to your own household or to a giant corporation, if you perform your job with competence you are needed and you are important.

Once, during a lecture to a high school psychology class, I was pressed by the students to single out what I deemed to be the highest calling for one to pursue in life. I told them that any work was the highest calling when performed with love and integrity. If I were to single out any specific fields for special honors, I told them, it would be farming and teaching. I went on to explain that teaching embraced all those who taught by the spoken or written word, or by visual effects: public school teachers; private school teachers; instructors in commercial schools; writers of books, articles, and stories; lecturers; parents; in short, anyone who spent time in earnest to enrich someone else by providing information or guidance.

The farmer enriches our bodies; the teacher, our minds. Together they enable us to grow, progress, and enjoy life.

After that lecture, one of the students approached me. He said, "Thank you for what you said about farmers. All my classmates poke fun at me for wanting to be a farmer like my father. They say I will just grow prematurely old from hard work and have nothing to show for it. But I love working the land and seeing things grow. It is like it is just me and God out there in the open field. We are partners in creating food for all His children. This may sound corny, but that is how I feel."

"No, you don't sound corny," I had told him. "You sound like a young man who is going to leave this world a better place for your having been here. If everyone approached their jobs with your attitude, the world wouldn't have any problems. Thank you for sharing your thoughts with me."

My daughter, Eileen, is a school teacher. When applying for a teaching position, she was asked to write her teaching philosophy. Here is what she wrote:

"My philosophy starts with the basic philosophy that any professional teacher ought to embrace. Namely: To contribute to humanity by helping enrich young minds so they can go forward and make their own contributions in whatever arena of life they so choose.

"I go a step further than this basic philosophy. In enriching young minds, I believe my greatest responsibility is to teach children to think and reason for themselves. I believe in helping children to become independent, not dependent.

"My approach to teaching is to create an atmosphere where children want to learn and are excited about learning. Learning is an interactive experience between teacher and students and among the students themselves. It is not a master/servant relationship where the teacher dictates and the student listens. Rather, it is a situation where the teacher is more of a coach, directing and participating, and where the students also participate as learning team members.

"I recognize the uniqueness and individuality of each human being. Therefore, I do not compare one child against another. I allow each child to be a full blown individual, and I compare that child only against his/her own potentials and achievements.

"My teaching skills are quite good, and I am always in charge of my classroom, without seeming to be the specter of an iron-fisted dictator. I wear a velvet glove.

"Of all the qualifications I take into my classroom every day, the most important is love. That is what makes it all work."

She got the teaching position!

So what job is best for you? What should you select for your life's work? The name of the occupation will vary with each of you, but one thing is certain.

When you can approach your chosen job with the love, excitement, and integrity that these two young people have expressed, you will have reached your highest calling.

Your choice of work is a very important building block for your bridge to tomorrow, so give it careful thought.

Like most people, you will probably have many different jobs in your life. Perhaps it will be a part-time job while going to school, or perhaps a temporary job at minimum wage in a fast food restaurant while trying to get situated in the line of work you really want. Perhaps fast food management is your goal. Perhaps you have had a series of various jobs due to layoffs, business bankruptcy, or whatever.

Here is just a sampling of some of the building blocks in my occupational bridge to my current destination as a professional writer: clerk in a drug store; retail shoe salesman; six years in the Air Force; electronic technician; executive with IBM; Kelly Girl (or perhaps Kelly Man is more correct); professional astrologer; professional hypnotherapist; technical writer consultant. Some of these jobs were part time. Some lasted many years, but the one goal I have had since I was a young boy in grade school was to be a professional writer. I never lost sight of that goal.

During all those jobs I had, I studied, took classes, and read books to teach myself and prepare myself to be a writer. I succeeded.

One important factor in succeeding was that I performed every job with excellence. I maintained a positive attitude and gave 100%.

As a shoe salesman, I memorized the entire stock, greeted every customer with a smile and a friendly word, and respected their right to not purchase anything if they didn't want to. I quickly became the store's top salesman.

During a recession period I was out of work, and I needed income to put bread on the table. Kelly Girl (now named Kelly Temporary Services) was advertising for office help, so I applied. They didn't want to hire me because I was a man. I persuaded them to at least give me the hiring tests, which they agreed to do although they were certain I would fail them. After all, what man could type sixty-five words per minute? What man could pass their English and spelling test?

Of course they didn't know that my dream was to be a writer. I had learned English, spelling, and typing as part of my preparation for being a writer. I "aced" the tests, so they reluctantly sent me out on a one-day assignment at minimum wage. They told me, "The customer might not even keep you the first day because they expect women to do this work."

That customer was so impressed with my attitude and 100% performance that he asked me to stay on for several more weeks to help set up a convention. Kelly Girl couldn't understand it.

I digressed to relate a couple of my personal experiences to illustrate three salient points about building your occupational bridge to tomorrow.

The first is attitude. No matter what your job is, do it with your whole heart. With zest. With enthusiasm. With the inner knowledge that you are a winner and deserve to be a winner.

Second—Give 100%, always. No exceptions. 99% is not good enough. A 99% bridge is not a sturdy one.

Third—Never give up. Never lose sight of your goal. Be persistent and determined. The following quotation attributed to Calvin Coolidge drives home this point more eloquently:

> *Press on. Nothing in the world can take the place of persistence. Talent will not; nothing is more common than unsuccessful people with talent. Genius will not; unrewarded genius is almost a proverb. Education alone will not; the world is full of educated derelicts. Persistence and determination alone are omnipotent.*

So what does all this mean to you?

It means that at any given moment in your life you are giving 100% to at least two different jobs: 100% to the job at which you are actually working at the time, and 100% to the job you will be doing when you reach the other side of your occupational bridge to tomorrow. That makes you a 200% person. You are capable of that. We all are capable of that.

What about when you get to the other side of your bridge? What then? At that time you will have grown more as a person. You will be more enlightened. You will know more and will have greater vision for your future.

At that time you will see other destinations for tomorrow, other bridges that you want to build, and you will start on yet another bridge to tomorrow.

And so it will go continuously, without end, because that is what life is all about. That is the essence and excitement of life. An endless chain of bridges to tomorrow. Each one more thrilling than the one before.

Chapter 10

# Altered States of Consciousness[1]

*The person who cannot wonder is but a pair of spectacles behind which there is no eye.*
Thomas Carlyle

Altered states of consciousness is one of the least understood and most misunderstood subjects that I deal with. Altered states are discussed in all my lectures, counseling sessions, and books. Many people regard altered states as some sort of aberration that is to be avoided. That is because they are forming their judgment from a vantage point of ignorance.

So I educate them.

There is no way one can avoid altered states of consciousness because everyone experiences altered states many times every day in a natural, normal, healthy way.

---

[1] This chapter is based on material in my book, *Hypnosis* (1986, Llewellyn Publications)

When you daydream you are in an altered state. When you go to sleep you cycle through several altered states. You dream in an altered state. When you awaken you cycle through altered states. While you are awake your brain frequently switches into an altered state for very short periods (a fraction of a second) to record experiences. For example, all emotion is recorded at an altered state called theta (more on this shortly). If you hit your thumb with a hammer, your brain switches to theta for a brief moment to record the pain. When you are attempting to memorize something, your brain automatically switches to an altered state called alpha to impress your memory with the data.

So altered states are a normal, natural, healthy phenomena.

You can learn to deliberately alter your state of consciousness and use that state for any beneficial purpose you desire. An altered state of consciousness is an especially effective tool for building bridges to tomorrow. That is why I have included this chapter.

My purpose here is to provide an accurate description of what altered states are, so you will be encouraged to use this great birthright to your advantage to enrich your life.

You have probably heard of mind-altering drugs, and that is where you may have gotten some apprehension about altered states. Yes, there are many drugs that will cause you to enter an altered state. Don't use them! Not ever! They are harmful to your mental and physical health. Also, you are not in control while in a drug-induced altered state. As a result, you are potentially harmful to yourself and to others. You have the illusion of being in control and of thinking great thoughts and of doing great things. But that is all it is . . . illusion. In reality, your thoughts in a drug-induced state range from trivia to garbage. Your actions range from stupid to detrimental. This is because you are not in control.

Conversely, in a naturally induced altered state, you are always in total control. Your thoughts are clear, intelligent, and often profound. Your actions are beneficial and intelligent. You are created this way. It is part of your birthright.

So, just what are the altered states of consciousness we all experience? Quite simply, they relate to the electrical frequency where our brain is functioning at any particular moment. The names of the states of consciousness are: beta; alpha; theta; and delta.

**Beta:** When our brain is operating at frequencies higher than fourteen cycles per second, we are said to be in the beta state. This is our normal, awakened state which relates to our conscious mind. In beta, we think, reason, rationalize, converse, go about our daily chores. On an average, our brain operates about twenty-two cycles per second for most of our awakened state functions.

If our brain were to rev up to sixty cycles per second, we would be in acute hysteria and out of control; some drugs can cause this to happen. Intense fear can also cause hysteria. Hysteria is an undesirable and sometimes dangerous state. By learning to control your own mind, you can prevent hysteria.

**Alpha:** In alpha, our brain operates between about seven cycles per second and fourteen cycles per second. This range is where we daydream and where we experience nocturnal dreams. On an average, our nocturnal dreams occur around ten cycles per second. At approximately ten cycles per second is also where rapid eye movement

(REM) occurs. Alpha is also the range where self-hypnosis takes place. Alpha is generally regarded as the range of the subconscious mind.

**Theta:** Theta is the four to seven cycle range of brain activity. This is the area where psychic awareness occurs. It is also the area where emotional experiences seem to be recorded.

**Delta:** Delta is below four cycles per second and is total unconsciousness. Very little is known about the nature and purpose of delta.

It is possible to deliberately alter your brain activity by perfectly normal, natural means without going to sleep. Then you are able to use those states of mind to achieve virtually anything you wish: to set goals; to get rid of unwanted habits (smoking for example); to engage in paranormal experiences; the list goes on endlessly. My book, *Hypnosis*, tells you how to achieve and use alpha. My book, *Beyond Hypnosis*, tells you how to achieve and use theta.

You do not have to be concerned about the frequency at which your brain is operating. All you need to do is to sit quietly where you have no distractions, close your eyes, breathe easily and rhythmically, and allow your mind and body to relax. As you relax, your mind will automatically adjust to the appropriate frequency. Once you are relaxed, you focus your mind on mental pictures and words that describe exactly what you want to occur.

This relaxed altered state puts you in direct communication with your subconscious mind and your higher mind where you can impress your desires, which your mind will then proceed to achieve.

For example, you want to build a bridge to find employment. While you are completely relaxed with your eyes closed you visualize yourself being interviewed for the job you want. You visualize being offered the job, which you accept. See yourself working happily on the job. Then with mental words, or out loud if you wish, state something like, "I want to find satisfactory employment within the next two weeks. I will find satisfactory employment because that is what I want and what I direct my mind to do for me. I am a successful person, and the job I am about to get will help me to be even more successful."

You can be much more elaborate in programming your mind than in my brief example. The idea is to use your subconscious mind and higher mind more fully in order to achieve whatever it is that you want. By altering your state of consciousness you engage a powerful tool to do just that.

Altered states of consciousness are a normal, natural, healthy, innate gift from our Creator. He gave them to us so we could vastly improve our lives and the lives of others, if we choose to do so.

Chapter 11, Self-Hypnosis, Meditation, and Prayer, expands a little further on the use of altered states of consciousness for building bridges to tomorrow.

Chapter 11

# Self-Hypnosis, Meditation, and Prayer[1]

*You must become something more than "mere man" on pain of becoming otherwise something less.*

A. E. Taylor

Self-hypnosis, meditation, and prayer are like triplets... nearly identical, with only subtle differences.

All three utilize the same altered state of consciousness, usually alpha, and all three put you in direct communication with Higher Mind.

The subtle difference between them is just in the purpose for which you use the altered state.

---

[1] This chapter is based on material in my book, *Hypnosis* (1986, Llewellyn Publications)

63

**Self-hypnosis:** This is the term generally used to indicate that you are using your altered state to solve problems; for example: to get rid of an unwanted habit; to define and set personal goals; to seek answers for problems; to allow your higher mind to feed you information that is needed or is beneficial. The list of uses is nearly infinite. Essentially, in this state, you give yourself positive suggestions to improve your life the way you want to improve it. For example you may program your mind with, "Everyday I am becoming a more confident and outgoing person," to aid you in overcoming shyness.

Your subconscious mind accepts your suggestions and turns them into reality in your life. That is one major purpose of your subconscious mind. Your subconscious mind is like an obedient servant; it does whatever you command it to do. The subconscious mind does not reason; it does not know positive from negative; it does not know right from wrong; it does not know best from worst. It just *does* whatever it is commanded to do.

A major reason that so many people have so many problems is that they have programmed their subconscious minds in the the wrong direction. Or, they have allowed others to program their minds for them in the wrong direction.

If a person is told over and over by parents, teachers, and peers that he/she is a lazy, stupid, worthless, no-good parasite on society, and if that person *accepts* those opinions as fact, then the person's subconscious mind will be so programmed, and it becomes reality. The person then does become a lazy, stupid, worthless, no-good parasite on society.

By properly using self-hypnosis, the person can redirect his/her life in a positive, constructive direction by reprogramming the subconscious mind in a constructive way.

Self-hypnosis is a powerful, proactive tool for creating your bridges to success and fulfillment.

Some examples of how I have used self-hypnosis on myself are: to get rid of headaches; stop pain from a wound; speed healing of a wound; gain self-confidence; improve my self-image; improve my memory; relax and get rid of stress; overcome fatigue when driving; program my mind with positive affirmations; past life regression; goal setting; and dozens of other things.

In addition, I have used hypnosis extensively on others for all of the above mentioned things, plus to help them: stop smoking; control eating (weight control); overcome fears and phobias; improve sexual functioning; overcome insomnia; suicide prevention; skill improvement of various kinds (typing, tennis, etc.); and much more.

Self-hypnosis is a skill that is very easy to learn and use, and I highly recommend it as a tool for building some of your bridges.

**Meditation:** This is the name generally used when the altered state is utilized for deep relaxation or for freeing yourself from your conscious mind to allow higher mind to enlighten you. In meditation you usually do not direct your subconscious to solve or achieve anything. Instead, you open yourself as a clear channel to receive enlightenment from cosmic mind.

I have received profound truth in meditation. The entire concept of reincarnation was given to me in meditation.

The great inventor, Nikola Tesla, was given the entire concept and design for the alternating current generator while in a relaxed, meditative state.

Much of this book (and my previous books) was given to me while I was in a meditative state. Meditation is a powerful tool for allowing your higher mind to feed you the information and awareness you need to build your bridges.

Some examples of how I use meditation are: to psychically send help to others; to psychically tune into higher mind to find information I need; to allow myself to receive information from cosmic consciousness; to forgive myself and others; to balance myself; and much more. For me, meditation is a powerful spiritual tool that takes up where hypnosis leaves off.

Through meditation I am able to extend my abilities to build bridges far in excess of my normal capability. I mentioned before that I get the information for my books primarily through an altered state of consciousness.

This is a powerful tool, but it does require practice, patience and persistence. It is something you may want to explore.

**Prayer:** Prayer is the name applied to the process of invoking the intercession of a supreme (usually considered divine) power.

Prayer, to be effective, needs to be done in an altered state of consciousness. Most people don't realize this fact; that is one reason why so many prayers seem to go unanswered. An unanswered prayer is not due to a capricious God. Not at all. True prayers are always answered. A prayer that seems to be unanswered is usually due to the one initiating the prayer not doing it properly, hence, not establishing a solid channel of communication. It is our responsibility to establish the channel to reach Divine Mind, and not vice versa.

One other reason for seemingly unanswered prayers is that the one praying doesn't recognize, or else rejects, the answer. More on this shortly.

In an altered state, one can easily contact the spark of divinity that our Creator endowed each of us with. Once you have gone deep within self and contacted your spark of divinity, your prayers become part of the total Divinity that is. Then you get results.

Those who spout elaborate oratory under the guise of prayer are merely putting on a show, nothing more. True prayer is an invoking within self that is born in the knowledge that we all possess divinity as a birthright from our Creator. Prayer need not be elaborate. The most powerful prayer I ever said was just one word. I was in a very difficult situation and was completely helpless to solve it. A man's life literally depended on my help, and I didn't know what to do. I altered my consciousness to alpha in an instant and mentally cried out to that divinity that is all and of which I am privileged to share, "Help!" That's all. Just, "help."

My help arrived instantly and in a way I could never have conceived. Some would call it a miracle. The problem was solved, and the man's life was saved. A complete, detailed account of this is in my book, *Beyond Hypnosis*. Prayer is a powerful tool for getting a higher power to help you build your bridges.

Let me close this chapter with a short story that illustrates an important aspect of prayer.

It seems that a raging storm caused a terrible flood, and the water was rising fast. The water rushed into a man's home, forcing him to take refuge on the second floor.

The water continued to rise until the man had to climb out onto the the highest peak of his roof to escape the relentlessly rising water.

He watched as the water inched up the roof, closer and closer. He began to pray.

Looking toward the heavens he cried out, "Lord, please save me from this flood!"

A few minutes later a helicopter flew over and hovered a hundred feet above the man. A rope was thrown from the helicopter so it hung down within the man's reach.

"Grab the rope and climb up!" a voice commanded over a bullhorn in the helicopter.

The wind was whipping the rope. The water current was swift and swirling. The man was terrified.

"No!" he called back. "I may fall before I could climb that far! It is too risky! I will wait for God to help me!" He waved the helicopter away.

The helicopter moved away to search for others who might be stranded, and the man once again called out to the heavens.

"Lord, please save me from this flood!"

Shortly a two-man rubber raft came paddling up. There were two men in it, and one called out, "Hey, Mac, slide down the roof into the water and we can take you aboard!"

The man assessed his situation. Three men might overload the little raft and he would be drowned. Or he might slide down into the water only to be swept away before the men in the raft could save him.

"No!" he yelled back. "It is too risky! I will wait for God to answer my prayer!" He waved the raft away, and they soon drifted out of sight.

Soon the water was lapping at his feet so he climbed

atop the chimney. "Lord!" he called out, "please help me now. I am almost a goner!"

He looked down and just six feet away a large log had snagged against the submerged rooftop. All he had to do was jump into the water and grab the log which was large enough to support him. But suppose he miscalculated his jump? Suppose he couldn't hold onto the log? It was too risky.

So he watched while the rising water eventually floated the log free and it drifted away.

The man was now standing on the chimney. Water had risen over the top of his feet. He knew he would die soon without help.

He turned once again to the heavens and cried out, "Lord, why have you not answered my prayers?"

And a voice from above answered back, "I sent you a helicopter, which you refused to accept. Then I sent you a raft that you refused to board. Finally I sent you a log, but you wouldn't use it. That is three strikes. You're out!"

There is a message in this story. If you pray, you can expect an answer. However, the answer may not be what you wanted. If you ignore the answer, you are on your own. The answer to a prayer will always be appropriate, but you are expected to accept some responsibility, too.

The man in the story was not willing to accept responsibility and take a calculated risk. He also was not willing to accept the answer to his prayers. He did not have enough faith in God to trust Him to supply the proper help.

God is willing to lend assistance, but He expects you to listen and to contribute to solving the problem, also.

If you want prayer to be an effective tool for you in building your bridges to tomorrow you must be sensitive enough to recognize the answer, then cooperate with the answer and do your part.

# Chapter 12

# Building a Bridge With Self Talk[1]

*The journey of a thousand miles begins with one step.*

Lao-Tse

Self talk is exactly what it sounds like: You talk out loud to yourself about whatever it is that you want. This is an extremely powerful tool for building bridges to tomorrow.

Self talk is my personal favorite method for bridge-building, and there is rarely a day that goes by without my using self talk for something. Frequently I use it in the morning to set the tone for the day. I will say out loud to myself something like, "Today is a great day and I will love every minute of it. Today my mind will be especially creative so I can conceive and write another chapter in the book I am writing." And so forth.

[1] This chapter is based on concepts developed in my book, *The Art of Self Talk* (1993, Llewellyn Publications)

You can cover a lot of ground in a short time by using self talk. I find that in ten to twenty minutes while driving to work in the morning, I can set the tone for the day, reaffirm all my major goals, set some goals for just that day, and reconfirm my personal creed and values.

Talking out loud to yourself is especially effective because:

1. It intensifies your concentration because it is difficult for your mind to wander aimlessly when you have to think about what you are saying.

2. In order to speak, you must first think, which doubles the effectiveness.

3. Then your ears hear the words you are saying, which go back into your brain for additional reinforcement.

4. Having to speak intelligent words and sentences causes your mind to crystallize the thoughts, impregnating them even deeper into your subconscious mind.

As you know by now, bridge-building is a matter of programming your subconscious mind with the information you want to cause a desired change or result in your life. Self talk works excellently for this.

There is virtually no limit to the uses of self talk in building bridges. Here are a few common uses just to give you an idea:

- Purchasing the exact new car you want at the price you want to pay, and not a "deal" that most benefits the dealer.

- Get a fair deal in general in any business transaction.

- Pass tests.

- Get the job, promotion, or salary increase you want.

- Chew yourself out effectively when you "goof up" so as to improve your behavior and performance.

- Improve your skills in anything (sports, typing, crafts, etc.).

- Throw constructive temper tantrums to let off steam and reduce stress.

- Keep yourself mentally and physically healthy.

- Overcome fears and phobias.

- Improve your memory.

- Set and achieve goals.

- Improve your love life.

- Establish a solid rapport with your boss, a prospective romantic interest, or other people in general.

- Program positive affirmations.

The list of possibilities is limited only by your own imagination to dream up the situation and words to program that situation.

The way it works is this: You instruct yourself out loud with the directions and information needed for you to achieve a desired goal.

For example, suppose your sexual performance with your wife has been disappointing lately. You love her, but have not been successful in getting yourself sufficiently aroused to perform. And on occasion your performance peaks and ends so fast your wife gets nothing out of the experience.

You analyze the situation. She has always been clean and fragrant and ready to make love. But you have been tired lately—too much stress at work and too much overtime work. When you get home you are sweaty and only want peace and quiet. You've been gulping down your dinner after which you plop in a chair, turn on the television, and drink a couple of beers. Then you doze off in the chair.

Instead of a bath or shower before bedtime, you say "I'll shower in the morning."

How fit are you to be a great lover at this time? You aren't fit at all, are you? Smelly, beer breath, groggy, and stressed out.

So you devise a self talk script to get yourself back on track. That script might go something like this.

In the morning you look into the mirror and say out loud to yourself:

"Hi, guy! Tonight I am going to once again be the great lover I used to be. Today at work I will not allow myself to get uptight with work. I will do the best I can, but I am not going to be upset if I make a mistake or don't get something done. There is always tomorrow to continue the work. And I will not stay late, working. At quitting time I will come home to my sexy wife, whom I love."

As you drive to work, visualize your wife looking lovely in her nightie, and say out loud, "I love you, hon, and tonight I am going to be your great lover again." Then rehearse the exact things you want to say to her that you know turn her on—say them out loud and allow them to arouse you also.

Follow this same pattern of visualization and talking out loud about these things during the day if you have a chance. Enroute home, repeat the words again and also add, "I will not crash out in front of the TV with beer tonight. No beer! No TV! Tonight is my love night with my wife. I will take a shower before going to bed and I will do and say all the things that turn us on. I will become aroused easily, and I will be able to perform for a long time so my wife will get maximum enjoyment."

You will find that you can build an effective love bridge using this self talk approach.

You can use self talk to help build any kind of bridge you want.

If you augment your self talk efforts with self hypnosis, meditation, prayers, astrology, attitude adjustment, and the other ideas presented in this book, you will have an extremely powerful and effective bridge-building program.

Talk it over with yourself and see what you think about it.

# Chapter 13

# Walk With Spirits

*Prayer is the contemplation of the facts of life
from the highest point of view.*
                    Ralph Waldo Emerson

The Indian, alone in his tepee, slowly rose to his feet. He was older in his heart than in his body. His frame was sturdy and his back as straight as the arrows of war that had darkened the sky for so many moons. He stepped to the entrance of his tepee and spoke a few soft words to the young brave standing in attendance outside.

While the brave went to fetch a pony, the Indian donned his headdress, reflecting briefly on the first time he wore this headdress many long winters ago when he was selected to be Chief of the Nez Perce and when the Great Spirit and the spirits of the ancient ones became his constant companions.

The Chief knew his people would be watching him intently, seeking some sign, hoping to hear some words of wisdom, waiting for some direction on what to do next. He must not let them see the weariness in his bones

or the pain of sadness in his heart. They must see their
Chief strong and resolute and wise.

He paused before exiting the tepee. He closed his
eyes, took a deep breath, and silently asked for strength.
A wash of energy filled him, pushing out the vestiges of
weariness.

A hundred pair of eyes outside watched their Chief
emerge from the tepee. His face was inscrutable. His
stride was strong and he looked neither right nor left as
he walked to the waiting pony. He deftly swung unas-
sisted onto the pony's back with the power and grace of
a young brave.

The Chief raised his right hand to shoulder height
with the back of his hand toward his people. He did not
want to be accompanied or followed. He urged the pony
forward at a slow trot toward the hill a short distance
from camp.

As the pony wended its way up the knoll, the
Chief could see his his camp at an oblique angle in the
distance below. Even from this distance the ravages of
war with the white man were evident to the Chief, not
because he had great eyesight but because he saw with
his heart. His people had been decimated. They were
sick. There was little to eat. They had fought valiantly,
but the white man had too many guns. The white man's
guns had driven them from their own land, on which
they and their ancestors had lived and hunted in harmony. There was little left except their dignity and their
indomitable spirit. Now the Chief must tell them what
to do next.

The Chief was a warrior of courage and fearless-
ness, and he would personally choose to fight to the
death. However, he was a Chief and he had a responsibility given to him by the Great Spirit. So he urged the

pony upward to the crest of the hill so he could consult with the ancient ones and with the Great Spirit.

Atop the hill, still astride his pony, the Chief bowed his head and his heart and closed his eyes. Even the pony lowered its head as though joining in meditation with its Chief.

The Chief allowed relaxation to flood his body. He allowed his mind to become empty to await communion with the spirits. The pony was motionless and made no noise. The evening sky stretched endlessly, spreading its quiet blanket across the land. No sound came from the Indian camp as they waited in a sort of silent prayer for their Chief to return.

The spirits came, and there was communion. The Chief's mind filled with their advice. The Chief now knew what he must do.

He opened his eyes, tilted his head back so he could gaze at the turquoise sky with orange fingers of the setting sun laced through the cloud puffs. He lifted his arms outstretched in a wide V, palms upward, toward the sky. His voice was strong and reverent as he spoke his prayer into the vastness of the universe:

"Hear me, my chiefs! I am tired. My heart is sick and sad. From where the sun now stands I will fight no more forever."

He then rode back to camp and repeated his prayer to his people and later to the world, when he surrendered to the white soldiers in order to bring peace to his people.

With those words in 1877, Chief Joseph of the Nez Perce changed the world of the American Indian and of the white man, and he joined the ranks of one of the truly great leaders of all time. Chief Joseph walked with the spirits, and in so doing achieved greatness. He built his bridge to peace and immortality.

Perhaps more than any other group of people, the American Indian understood, and understands, the sacred relationship between themselves, the earth, the wind, the creatures, their ancestors and other spirits, and their God. They walked with spirits and created a legacy for all mankind to learn from.

Though penned up, pushed down, cheated, lied to, and defiled by the white man and his laws, the American Indian has survived with dignity, courage, and honor. From them, we can learn.

Those of us who are non-Indian but who also walk with spirits will, like the Indian, survive with dignity, courage, and honor, and will readily see the modern day parallels of our spirituality to that of the American Indian.

Those of us who are non-Indian and who do not walk with spirits can learn to do so if we choose. In so doing, we can achieve greatness in our own little way.

True greatness walks hand in hand with the spirits. Not all great people are famous or end up in history books, but all great people walk with spirits. Plumbers, teachers, farmers, accountants, lawyers, laborers, *ad infinitum* can achieve greatness in their own way, because greatness is born in the heart in communion with the spirits. Most of us will never do great things, but we can walk with spirits and do small things in a great way.

Walking with spirits means to establish a communion, an interaction, a communication with higher intelligence sources in the universe and to live and act in harmony with that higher wisdom.

What a marvelous source of help and guidance for building our bridges to tomorrow!

Today many of us walk with spirits in a similar manner as did Chief Joseph. Through self-hypnosis, meditation, and prayer we have communion with higher mind or cosmic consciousness and become enlightened or helped in some way. The American Indians innately knew about life after death, communicating with spirits, the use of crystals, stones, fetishes, herbs and all those other things associated with what we in our highly advanced civilization call *New Age*.

We are now learning anew what has been known for centuries. It surely is true that the more things change, the more they remain the same.

What you do about your own personal life after you read this book is your choice alone, but you will at least be armed with a new, valuable perspective from which to develop your choices and to build your bridges to tomorrow.

# Chapter 14

# Don't Run, Walking is Better

*The tragedy of the world is that people have given first class loyalty to second class causes and these causes have betrayed them.*
                                        Lynn Harold Hough

You have probably heard the story about the airline pilot who got on the intercom system to make an announcement to his passengers.

"Folks," he said, "I have some good news and some bad news."

"The good news is that we have a strong tailwind and are making excellent time. The bad news is that we are lost."

A great many people go through life just like that airplane pilot. They are making great time, covering a lot of territory, but they aren't getting anywhere.

For a pilot to be successful, he/she must know the destination and must arrive at the destination.

To be successful in life we must know where we are going, and we must take steps to assure our arrival at our desired destination. One way to do that is to build bridges to tomorrow.

Coherent thought is required to build bridges that are sturdy and that reach the desired goal. Coherent thought is generally incompatible with speed. Did you ever try to solve a math problem, or memorize a speech or poem, or plan a corporate reorganization, or analyze data while running a foot race at full speed against a time limit? Probably not, because it is close to impossible to do it.

When there is a problem to be solved what do most people do? They either sit quietly and think or they take a leisurely walk while they think. They do not take off on a dead run to think things over, do they?

Yet when it comes to the business of living, many people race through life hell-bent for election, in ten directions at the same time. Their daily itinerary reads like an airline flight schedule. They are so busy coming and going, attending this function and that function, meeting with this person or that person, doing this and doing that, running, running, running, busy, busy, busy, that they don't have time to think about who they are, what they are doing, or where they are heading. Their lives are filled with quantity of activity but not necessarily quality of activity.

Is it any wonder that we have so many mental breakdowns, physical breakdowns, drug and alcohol addiction, and suicides? Happy, truly successful people don't have these kinds of problems.

"Of course I am happy!" says Mr. or Ms. Busy. "I am an executive with my company. I work twelve hour days and attend ten meetings a day to conduct company business, and I travel two weeks a month to represent my company. In addition, I am a member of three private clubs, am president of the PTA, play golf every Sunday, and go bowling every other Thursday night. This is in addition to my role as a parent and spouse. And I am active in my political party." All external activities, are they not? Where is there time for internal activities for themselves?

Does the preceding scenario sound familiar? Of course, the specifics vary from person to person, but we all know someone who is Mr. or Ms. Busy. Perhaps you are a Mr. or Ms. Busy.

Is "overly busy" or "fast" the same as "happy" or "successful?" I doubt it. Have you ever seen a racehorse stop to smell the roses? Have you ever tried to smell a rose while on a dead run? It can't be done, can it?

How much scenery can you enjoy if you are going fast? Little if any because your attention must be focused completely on your forward movement.

When you hit just the right amount of "busy" and just the right rate of speed, then you can be exceptionally happy. I suggest for your consideration that the right amount of "busy" should leave some quiet time for you, and not be 100% occupied with burning up your time to satisfy external activities. I also suggest that the best rate of speed is a walk, not a run.

When you walk it is easy to pause and smell the roses or drink in the scenery.

And most importantly, the only way you can build reliable bridges is to internalize your thoughts and take time to think coherently about yourself, who you are, what you are doing, and where you want to go.

Nice and easy does it every time—remember the fable about the race between the tortoise and the hare. The tortoise won.

In Chapter 8 I talked about serendipity, which is the faculty of making fortunate and unexpected discoveries by accident. The only people who have serendipity in their lives are those people whose pace of living is organized enough so they have the time to recognize a serendipitous moment and take advantage of it.

Millions of people have serendipitous moments presented to them, but they never recognize them because their pace of living is so fast or hectic that they zip by the moment unaware. You cannot read house numbers while driving down a street at 100 miles per hour. Likewise, you cannot read life's many signposts while racing through life so fast that all your attention is focused on your forward motion so you don't run into something.

Don't be one of those people who suddenly realizes that their children are now adults and they have no clear, poignant memories of their childhood because they were too busy with other activities.

When you live too fast a pace—busy for the sake of being busy—you set the stage for a life of regrets because in retrospect you will clearly see your missed opportunities. You will see when you had serendipitous moments that you never followed up. Like driving so fast that you missed the turnoff to the right road, you will miss life's turnoffs to the right road for your life.

Let me tell you a true story that happened to me that shows very clearly the advantage of being a "walker" rather than a "runner" in life.

In 1966 I was promoted to manager of a technical publications department in IBM. I have always been a "walker." I spent time planning my department's operation. I made it a point to get to know all the people reporting to me. I mean *really* getting to know them. I knew their spouses names and occupation, their children's names and ages, their goals, gripes, recommendations, skills, problems, and so forth. They became like a second family. I did this because I realized the truth that it would be them, not me, who made our department the best it could be.

Every week I made it a point to stop and chat with everyone in my department one-on-one.

I also cultivated good relationships with the fellow managers with whom I regularly interacted, in order to facilitate harmonious cooperation.

I found the time to do these things by refusing to attend meetings that I felt were not important to my goals. In management there are always an endless succession of meetings to attend, and unfortunately most managers succumb to the trap of spending all their time in meetings. I also delegated everything possible to my people, and I empowered them to make decisions. I kept a low profile.

As a result, I was unhurried and happy. My people were engaged in meaningful work with the power to make most of their own decisions. They were happy and exceptionally productive. I made sure they received all the salary increases and promotions they earned.

One of my peers was also a newly appointed manager of another department. He was a "runner." I shall call him "Whiz."

Whiz never missed a meeting regardless of whether it was beneficial or not. He wanted to maintain high visibility for himself among "the powers that be."

When Whiz wasn't in a meeting you could see him racing down the hallway, coat tails flying, a sheaf of papers in his hand, on his way to or from someplace.

If anyone other than a top manager tried to stop him in the hall to ask him something he would say, "Later. I am in a hurry right now," and he would keep on moving.

The one place you would never find Whiz was in his own office or in his own department area. He was too busy going places, tending to details that could be better handled by his people. His people were unhappy. They didn't receive the salary increases or promotions they should have had, because Whiz had no idea what they were doing. He barely knew who they were.

Whiz seemed to be every place at once, making himself known, because he wanted to be recognized and promoted to a higher level of management.

One day, our IBM plant of about 6,000 people was given an extensive survey by an independent company, at the request of our corporate management. Top management wanted to know where the problems were, who was happy and why, who was unhappy and why, which departments were doing well, which departments were doing poorly, who were the best or the worst managers, and so forth.

At a subsequent "all managers" meeting we were given the results of the survey. I was highly praised by our laboratory director because I had the highest rated department, and had received the highest rating as a manager.

Whiz, as you have probably guessed, was rated the poorest manager and had the poorest department rating. In the next two years I was promoted twice into executive management. Whiz was removed from management and transferred to another plant.

Point made!

If you are a racehorse, slow down. Build a bridge to more orderliness in your life. Reassess your priorities. Sensitize yourself to be aware of, and enjoy, each moment of your life at the moment you experience it. Stop being overly concerned about schedules and external "busy" things. Take time for yourself so you can think coherently about yourself, your goals, your bridges to success and fulfillment, today and tomorrow.

Stop running. Walking is better.

L

# Chapter 15

# Spirituality

*It is not easy to find happiness in ourselves,*
*and it is not possible to find it elsewhere.*
Storm Jameson

Spirituality covers a broad spectrum of beliefs and practices dealing primarily with the non-physical aspects of life such as: truth, God or other deity, brotherhood of mankind, religion, oneness, cosmic consciousness, life and death, heaven and hell, karma; retribution, forgiveness, sin, evil, goodness, revenge, and so forth.

Spirituality concerns what goes on in our minds, thoughts, and hearts. Our philosophy of life. Our general conduct and behavior. Our creed that we live by. Our perception of who we are and how we fit into the total scheme of life. Our relationship with our creator.

Spirituality is not a quality that can be defined in specific terms because it is a fluid attribute that we can each tailor to our own desire. One person may believe in one supreme God. Another may believe there is no God at all, but does believe in the brotherhood of man.

Another believes in life eternal. Another that the grave is the end. Another in cosmic consciousness. Another in the dogma of a specific religious sect. And so on. There probably are no two people in the world whose spirituality is exactly 100% the same. There is no right or wrong to this. It is just the way it is.

As a person grows, experiences, and learns, he/she has the flexibility to alter their spirituality to suit them, and they most likely will do so to some extent even if only in a minor way.

In building your bridges to tomorrow it is important to know what your spirituality is, how to change it, and when to change it so as to ensure the most fulfilling life for yourself.

Some people are totally devoid of spirituality. Sociopaths are an example. Without spirituality, one automatically builds a bridge to destruction of self, and frequently of other innocent people also. The destruction of others may be literal (i.e., murder) or it may be symbolic. Some examples of symbolic destruction might be: deliberately lying about someone to prevent them from getting a raise or promotion; destroying or altering records to get someone in trouble; deliberately ignoring a plea for help from someone in distress, and so forth.

A person can be an atheist and still be spiritual. For example, the atheist who helps someone in distress is committing a spiritual act. So do not make the common mistake of thinking that spirituality and religion are synonymous. They may be synonymous in some people and mutually exclusive in other people. Spirituality is a unique state of being for each of us.

I view spirituality as having either of two aspects: 1) unstructured spirituality or 2) structured spirituality, of which religion is a subset. I shall discuss both of these aspects so you will have more perspective to help you build your own spiritual bridge if you choose to do so.

## *Spirituality*

First, unstructured spirituality. These are people who usually do not affiliate with a specific spiritual organization such as a religious sect. They do not want the structured rules and dogma of an established organization to dictate how they behave or how they interact with a higher spiritual intelligence (i.e., God, Cosmic Consciousness, Higher Mind, Higher Self, etc.).

These people believe in the brotherhood of mankind in a very special way. They see themselves as individual universes unto themselves and see all other people as individual universes also. Their primary goal is to interact with all others in the most harmonious and beneficial way they possibly can.

They believe they alone are responsible for their destiny and that their creator has endowed them with the ability to create their own reality. They interact with higher intelligence through their own meditation, prayer, talk, or thought in accordance with their own rules and beliefs.

Occasionally they may meditate in concert with others, but it is an unstructured way with each person doing their own thing.

- The person who meditates and visualizes a sick person being healed is practicing unstructured spirituality.

- The person who uses self-hypnosis to overcome an undesirable trait is practicing unstructured spirituality.

- The person who gives himself/herself positive affirmations is practicing unstructured spirituality.

- The person who talks out-loud to his/her perceived God is practicing unstructured spirituality.

In other words, when a person interacts beneficially with self, others, or deity in a self-directed manner and not in accordance with dogma that someone else has dictated, he or she is practicing unstructured spirituality. They feel free to practice their spirituality any time, any place.

The advantage of this type of spirituality is that you alone control your life without outside influence. You accept full responsibility and you do not feel let down by others.

The disadvantage is that you do not have the mutual supportiveness of a group or organization whose spirituality can often bolster your own.

### *Structured*

Structured spirituality is the practice of one's personal beliefs within the confines of the rules and dogma of an organization. Most often these are religious organizations or fraternal organizations.

The organization specifies certain rules to be followed, rituals to be practiced, ceremonies to be performed, and even has a list of dos and don'ts that classify certain acts as either being acceptable or unacceptable. Often they specify certain prayers to be said or songs or chants to be sung. They set certain times or days during which to practice spiritual activities.

If the organization believes that a certain practice is evil or harmful, then the members must accept that as their own belief also. Conversely, if the organization believes that a certain practice is good, the members must accept that as their own belief.

The advantage of structured spirituality is that it offers the supportiveness of others. It also frees you from accepting full responsibility for yourself because you allow the organization to be responsible for deciding what you will believe and what you won't believe.

The disadvantage is that you lose a portion of your freedom and individuality.

In comparing unstructured spirituality and structured spirituality there is no "best" for everyone. There is only what is best for you at a given moment in your life, and only you can make that determination.

It is not possible to estimate accurately how many people practice unstructured spirituality, but we can get a reasonable estimate about structured spirituality because most of these people are members of some religious sect.

There are literally thousands of organized religions and sub-sects of those religions. To mention a few of the more prominent ones: Moslem, Jewish, Christian, Hindu, Taoism, Buddhism, Confucianism, Wicca, Spiritualist, and on and on.

Because religion represents a major segment of spirituality, let's examine religion in more detail in a generic way.

## *Religion*

One of the definitions the dictionary gives for religion is: "institutionalized system of religious attitudes, beliefs, and practices." It is within this context that this chapter discusses religion.

As far back as 1972, my meditations have brought me awareness that institutionalized religion as we currently know it has reached its peak and is on the wane. Within the next several generations these venerable institutions purportedly dedicated to God may cease to exist. The erosion has already started.

The reasons for the potential collapse of these institutions are many and complex. I'll cover a few of the major ones in a simplistic way in order to make you aware. Then you can observe, use your own meditations, and arrive at your own conclusions as to what you want to do in your own best interests.

1. These institutions really are profit-making corporations. For tax purposes they are regarded as being non-profit, charitable organizations, but in reality they are not. They couldn't survive in their current structure without making a profit.

2. Most of these institutions do return some of the money to the people in various forms of relief or charity. But, like any large corporation, there is tremendous expense: buildings, land holdings, investments, salaries, pomp and ceremony, public relations, lobbying, television time, travel expenses, and so forth. What is left for charity is dwarfed by the overhead expense. If you give one dollar directly to a needy person, that person receives one dollar's worth of help. If you give one dollar to a religious institution, the needy person will be lucky indeed to see a nickel's worth of it.

3. These institutions constantly fight among themselves and bicker internally. They all have different sets of rules, and yet they all claim to be the one true voice of God. When is the last time you heard God bicker and fight? Have you ever heard of God giving conflicting rules for you to follow?

4. At least half our population is female, yet most of these institutions regard women as second class citizens. Women are not allowed to be part of the clergy in most religions. I didn't know God discriminated, did you?

5. These institutions are rigidly structured to maintain control of power, keep their members "in line," make a profit, and not allow "new thought" to enter the hallowed halls of their sanctimonious buildings.

6. For centuries, these institutions have (deliberately, I think) kept their members in ignorance by forbidding them to think or do anything that is not specifically sanctioned in the institution's rigid dogma. If the institution did not want its members to learn about something, it was labeled as evil or sinful.

7. The effect of the institutions' actions is to prevent its members from realizing the full joy of freedom that God gave them as a birthright. Members are kept in a subservient, restricted role.

These seven reasons are only the tip of the iceberg. All of these reasons are the institutions' own doing. They have set the stage for their own demise.

The demise will occur because people are becoming more aware and more conscious of their innate right to joy, freedom, and expression. People are growing weary of being told how to think; they want to think for themselves. They are tired of hearing that everything is sinful. They are beginning to question everything instead of blindly accepting everything. What is evil about dancing? What is wrong with wearing cosmetics? Why is it wrong to get a divorce when the marriage is a disaster? Why am

I condemned if I don't attend Sunday church services? And so on go the questions that people are asking.

To be fair, these institutions have done a lot of good. They were, and still are, a binding force to unite people in a common strength and cause to stand against any oppression from governments. They were a significant force in aiding people to obtain more freedom than governments would otherwise have allowed.

It is ironic that people will now start deserting these institutions because they perceive the institutions as depriving them of their complete freedom. And the people will be right in their assessment.

Religion, in its broadest, purest sense is the relationship between an individual and God. This will always be with us and will never change. It is just that people are becoming more aware that they may be able to explore their relationship with God much more effectively and satisfactorily on their own outside the institutionalized structure. This awareness and exploration has already begun, and its tempo will quicken at an ever-increasing rate over the next several generations.

Without support, the institutions may wither and vanish. When this book is printed and distributed, my name will become anathema in many religious circles. I will be decried from pulpits. This is often the price one must pay for speaking the truth. So be it.

What does this have to do with you or with building a bridge to tomorrow? Plenty!

Religion, when boiled down to its basic meaning, means simply "a person's personal belief system." Your personal belief system may be in a supreme being who you call God, Allah, the Great Spirit, Cosmic Consciousness, or whatever.

- Your personal belief system may be that there is no supreme being.

- You may believe that you can best serve your own needs by worshiping in an established institution.

- You may believe that you can best serve your own needs by being spiritual in your own personal way; just you and God.

- You may believe that you alone are all that is important; that there is no higher intelligence.

Whatever you believe, dedicate yourself to your beliefs. By doing so you have clear direction in life and thus can contribute to yourself and to the world.

Spend some time in serious meditation about your beliefs. Be sure you are certain what is best for you. Whatever your spiritual belief is, it should serve you so you can realize the joy, peace, progress, and success in life that you want. If it does, then stick with it and support it. If it doesn't, then look for a belief system that does fulfill your needs.

Earlier in this chapter I pointed out what may cause the disintegration of current religious institutions. If you choose to be a part of one of these institutions, then start now to build a bridge within your institution to restore its servitude to God and to its members rather than to the almighty dollar and to corporate (power) interests. The demise of religious institutions can be prevented if enough people build bridges to make the necessary changes.

Whatever spiritual bridge you build, keep your future options open. Be aware that tomorrow you may be more enlightened, may be more knowledgeable, may have experiences that may impel you to want to change. If so, don't hesitate to build a new spiritual bridge. Be flexible.

You may choose to express and develop your spirituality within some established religious sect. Hundreds of millions do this, and there is nothing wrong with that. It is an honorable way to dedicate and express yourself. It is possible to attain great spiritual growth this way.

It is also possible to attain great spiritual growth by developing yourself through an unstructured spiritual path of meditation, self-direction, and mental interaction with higher intelligence and universal consciousness.

And there are some who will find that they want to pursue both a structured and an unstructured spiritual path simultaneously. That is great!

I offer the thoughts in this chapter to make you think. I want to shake you out of your mental lethargy. Thinking is the hardest work there is, which is probably why so few engage in it.

I have deliberately not discussed my own personal spiritual beliefs because I do not want to imply that my way is the best way for you. My way is best for me at this moment in time.

I just want you to shake the cobwebs from your mind and think for yourself. What is best for you? Where do you want to go in life? What belief system serves you best? What spiritual bridge will take you to the joy, fulfillment, success, peace, and freedom you want?

When you decide, then build the bridge.

After you cross your bridge you should find happiness, peace, freedom, success, and fulfillment. If you don't find those things, then you have built the wrong bridge. You will then need to seriously reassess who you are and what you should do in your own best interests. Then build a new spiritual bridge.

# Chapter 16

# Change

*Life is a series of surprises, and would not be worth taking or keeping if it were not.*
Ralph Waldo Emerson

Change is often desirable, frequently necessary, and always inevitable. The only thing constant in life is change, so be prepared to change if your awareness takes a new direction. That is how we grow—by flowing in harmony with change, and putting ourselves in charge of making change happen in our lives.

That is why bridge-building is so important. By building bridges, you take control of the changes in your life. Notice that in this book I do not talk about just one bridge to tomorrow, I talk about multiple bridges. I even talk about destroying bridges and building new ones when the old one isn't taking you where you want to be. This is necessary because change is a constant companion to all of us.

You change. As you mature, learn more, get more experience, you change your values, your interest, and your goals. It is a never ending process.

Your environment changes, and you must respond to it. The state builds a highway next to your house. Your living area becomes polluted. A flood wipes you out. And so forth.

Living conditions change, requiring you to readjust your life. You lose your job. War breaks out. You get married or divorced. Children are born and eventually leave home. A death in the family. Health problems.

If you learn to handle change, you can survive anything and keep on progressing. You can learn to plan and execute your own changes so as to keep your life headed in the direction you want.

Yet most people have a dreaded fear of change. They see change as a threat to their well being. In reality change often opens the door for greater opportunity.

Let's examine one common kind of change and see what sort of reactions one might have to it—suddenly losing your job. This is one change that I have had a lot of personal experience with.

The company announces that the economic downturn has forced them to layoff 20% of their employees immediately. It is unexpected. Joe Gloom is one who got his "pink slip."

"The world has ended!" is Joe Gloom's reaction. I am forty-five years old. I have twenty years with the company. What can I do now? Nothing! If I am lucky, I might get a part-time job at minimum wage in a fast food restaurant."

So Joe Gloom heads straight for a barroom and gets drunk, spending every cent in his pocket, which worsens his situation. I've seen this sort of reaction to change many times, and I'll bet you have, too.

The saddest case I personally know of happened in early 1982 when I was writing procedures for a company in the oil shale business. The company was one that hired as many physically handicapped people as they could because they were good corporate citizens. The oil shale "crash" forced massive layoffs, of which I was one. One of the layoffs was a young draftsman whose legs were severely crippled due to a birth defect. He went home that day and put a bullet through his head.

That day I went home and told my wife we were taking a three-month motor home vacation. We were packed up and on the road in less than a week.

What a contrast in reactions to the same situation. The young man took his life, and I took a vacation.

I am a consummate bridge-builder, so I take things in stride and make them work for me, not against me.

Twice I worked for fledgling start-up companies in the electronics design and manufacturing business. Both companies went bankrupt, locking their doors without notice, leaving hundreds of people without employment and without wages due them.

In both cases I escaped unscathed just a couple months before the end because I built a bridge to another job and quit in order to accept another employment offer. Was this dumb luck? No, it wasn't. The signs of pending bankruptcy were much in evidence for anyone who cared to notice. I noticed and acted accordingly. My friends would not believe my analysis, so they stayed with the company and lost their job and their back wages.

In Chapter 14, I advised you to walk, not run. My friends in the preceding situation were runners, and they didn't notice what was happening around them. I have always been a walker so I am able to absorb what is going on. You will have a much better chance of anticipating change and reacting to it if you are a walker.

The better job you can do to anticipate change, the better job you can do to build a bridge to take advantage of the opportunities the change brings.

In those cases where change is thrust on you suddenly and unexpectedly, you need to force yourself to accept the change for what it is and deal with it by examining all the facts involved. Then you need to seek whatever opportunity there may be as a result of the change. It may be an opportunity to learn a valuable lesson, an opportunity to learn new skills, an opportunity to relocate to another area, an opportunity to grow as a person, or whatever. The opportunity is there, but it isn't always readily available; you may need to search for it.

In summary, think of change and life as being synonymous. They go hand in hand. The following is a true story of how one man dealt with the most disruptive and unwelcome of all changes—the death of a loved one.

George Burns, the irrepressible comedian-actor, and his comedienne-actress wife, Gracie, are one of the great love stories of all time. Their love and devotion to each other was unsurpassed. They lived for each other, and their comedy act was a show business legend.

Then at the pinnacle of their professional career, Gracie dropped dead. Suddenly. Unexpectedly.

George was devastated. A lesser man would have been finished then and there. This was a change thrust on George without warning. He didn't want it, but he had it anyway and he had to deal with it.

George is a bridge-builder. He looked for what he could salvage from this personal disaster. He had one thing—his undying love for Gracie, and the strength he could muster because of that love. Gracie was with him spiritually every moment of every day.

Armed with this great love, he picked himself up and went on to become a great living legend in show business. At this writing, George is nearly 100 years old and is still performing to standing room only audiences.

George is a giant of a man, though small in physical stature, who knows how to build bridges that successfully deal with change.

Accept change, don't fear it. Make change work for you, not against you. Learn to orchestrate changes in your life so you achieve what you want.

Change can be managed and directed when you become a consummate builder of bridges to tomorrow.

Learn to change your thinking, and you can change your life.

# Chapter 17

# Natal Astrology[1]

*I shall be telling this with a sigh*
*Somewhere ages and ages hence;*
*Two roads diverged in a wood, and I,*
*I took the one less traveled by*
*And that has made all the difference.*

Robert Frost

I am an astrologer, and I meet two kinds of people. There are those who seek me out and solicit my services to help them improve their lives in some way through astrological counseling. And then there are those who think I am an idiot for believing in astrology.

This chapter is written for both of these kinds of people. I'll briefly explain what astrology is and what it is not in simple, non-technical language. I'll discuss what astrological counseling is and how you can use this powerful tool to your advantage. There are many different types of astrology, each with its own special purpose.

---

[1] This chapter in part is taken from my book, *Astrology for Beginners* (1992, Llewellyn Publications)

This chapter is confined to natal astrology, which is my specialty. Natal astrology deals with the birth patterning of individuals.

At this point you are probably asking yourself, "What does astrology have to do with building a bridge to tomorrow?"

The answer is: Natal astrology enables you to learn more about yourself, which is essential for building strong bridges. Continue reading and this will become more apparent.

Astrology is just one of many tools we have at our disposal to help us deal with problems and enrich our lives. Some other tools are: self-hypnosis; meditation; prayer; education. Like all tools, astrology gets the job done when understood and used properly.

**What natal astrology is:**

1. A tool that provides greater understanding of self.

2. The oldest empirical science in the world.

3. A patterning of a person's innate birth potentials, strengths, weaknesses, tendencies, probabilities. Intelligent information is available on every aspect of a person's life from cradle to grave.

**What natal astrology is not:**

1. It is **not** a cure all.

2. It is **not** fatalistic. The individual always has the ability to choose by exercising the birthright of free will.

3. It does **not** advocate that the planets control our lives. We, through our choices, control our own lives.

## The Philosophy of Astrology

I do not personally know any astrologer who thinks that planets cause events in our lives.

We astrologers believe in the oneness of the universe and in the dependence, interdependence, interaction, and mutual reflectiveness of everything with everything.

Astrology is based on the observation that events here on earth are instantly reflected in the heavens. A simplistic analogy might be this: If you look into a mirror while trimming your eyebrows and you accidentally pierce your skin with the scissors, you will instantly see the wound bleeding in the mirror. The mirror did not cause the wound or the bleeding, did it? The mirror accurately reflected an event at the precise time the event occurred.

If it were possible to have a mirror that looked ahead in time, you could have seen the accident ahead of time and thus avoided it by exercising more care or by not trimming your eyebrows at that time.

In astrology, the heavens, i.e., the planetary positions and movements, are our mirror of earthly events. Nearly five thousand years of careful observation and record keeping have supplied us with accurate knowledge as to what kinds of earthly events are associated with what kinds of heavenly patterns.

Our astrological mirror is superior to our bathroom mirror because the planets' patterning is constantly changing. The planets and their relationships to each other and to the earth change unendingly in an absolutely predictable way. We can mathematically calculate exactly where every planet will be at any time for any point on earth. This means we have a mirror that can reflect events in the past, present, or future anywhere on earth. An awesome thought, is it not?

This powerful tool was given to us as part of creation. The planets were created as part of our world for our use. The science of astrology strives to understand and use this great gift for the benefit of humanity.

Even though it is five thousand years old, astrology is still in its infancy. The planet Pluto, for instance, was only discovered in February, 1930, and it is still being studied. Who knows what all is out there to provide us even more information?

Still, a great deal of valuable, useful information is known and can be used to enrich our lives and help us to make better decisions and choices.

It works this way. Suppose your birth occurred at 6:44 p.m. EST, on March 31, 1960, in Kingston, New York. The astrologer figures out mathematically where the Sun, Moon, and the eight known planets were at that moment with respect to that specific geographic point on earth. He/she determines that your natal Sun is at eleven degrees and fifteen minutes of Aries in your sixth house; your Moon is at five degrees and seven minutes of Gemini in your eighth house; and so forth for the remaining eight known planets.

The astrologer then enters the information onto a circular map known as a horoscope chart which shows your unique horoscope patterning. He/she then studies the hundreds of factors in the patterning and compiles the data into a report known as your natal horoscope analysis. This report can tell virtually everything about all aspects of your life as were reflected at your birth moment in the mirror of the heavens.

This kind of natal horoscope report can be greatly beneficial. Suppose, for example, you were unsure of what career path to pursue. Your chart will tell you which pursuits you have the best chance of being successful in, and then you can make a choice based on this knowledge, rather than just shooting blindly in the dark.

Predictive astrology is similar to natal astrology, except that predictive astrology looks at a future date and analyzes your options at that time. This knowledge can help you avoid or lessen problems and take better advantage of opportunities.

What can astrology do to enhance a person's life? Let's examine three of the most dominant factors in the life of a person: companionship; career; and time.

**Companionship.** An astrologer can do a compatibility analysis between any two people and very accurately delineate the positive and negative aspects of a given relationship. The axiom "forewarned is half armed" really applies here. The more you know about the compatibility (or incompatibility) between you and another person, the better equipped you are to interact with that person to your benefit.

I did a compatibility analysis for a young lady who was going to marry a man she was certain she was deeply in love with. Their horoscope charts showed that the mutual attraction was totally physical, very strongly so, and that they had virtually nothing else in common. In addition, his chart showed a violent temper and a sadistic nature. In spite of this, she chose to marry him.

Within a few weeks after the marriage, he beat her brutally. Fortunately, she remembered my warning and left him before he could hurt her further. Astrology clearly showed her the probabilities and choices, but the choice was hers alone to make.

One can wisely use this feature of astrology to improve chances of having a harmonious and happy relationship. Relationship applies not only to marriage, but also to romance, friendship, business, or any sort of partnership.

But in any situation, it is the individual's choice that directs the events, not the planets'. The planets show the parameters involved and the likely result of choices. But always, the individual's choice prevails. This is the least understood, and most important factor in astrology. Astrology is not fatalistic at all. The individual is in charge. The horoscope chart shows the potentials; the individual makes the choices.

**Career.** I have already mentioned briefly that your chart can identify your innate talents, strengths, and abilities. Often a person selects a career path because of money, family tradition, or just by chance. Rarely do these careers produce self-fulfillment. It is much better to select a career that takes advantage of what you have to offer and of your interests.

I did an analysis for a thirty-eight year old bachelor. He was grossly unhappy with every aspect of his life. His chart showed why. He was a mediocre, bored electronics engineer, yet his chart very strongly indicated that law enforcement was his strong talent.

He readily admitted that since he was a young boy he had wanted to be a policeman; but peer and parental pressure to select a career that paid well influenced him to become an engineer. His chart showed a slight ability for engineering, hence he could do it, but it wasn't even close to being his strong suit. In addition, his chart indicated a strong materialistic streak. It also showed a love of children and a desire for marriage. He chose to let materialism dominate him; as a result he drove women away rather than attract them.

If he had had his horoscope done years earlier, he would have clearly seen his probabilities and options and might have made some different choices to ensure his happiness.

**Time.** Many people burn up time in unproductive pursuits just to keep busy and kill excess time. Others pine away their time in loneliness. Neither situation has to be that way.

Everyone is so multi-faceted in talent and interests that there is plenty of self-fulfilling activity to be engaged in. Most people do not realize this truth. They go through life as one-dimensional persons because they haven't discovered their multi-dimensional nature.

A horoscope chart and analysis will clearly show each person's depth, talents, abilities, etc. Armed with this knowledge, it becomes easy to select extra-curricular activities that are fulfilling and worthwhile, whether it be a hobby, avocation, second career, volunteer work, travel, or whatever. Again astrology presents the options . . . you make the choice.

Some may choose to become amateur astrologers. This will eat up as much time as you choose to devote, and it is an excellent way to get to know yourself in greater depth and to know, understand, and meet people.

There is nothing magic about this process. It is all based on what *is*; on fact, on calculations, and on interpretation by a qualified person.

The skill of the astrologer is the only weak link in the chain. A good astrologer will erect an accurate chart and interpret it accurately. An unskilled or careless astrologer will not do a good job.

But this isn't unique to astrology, is it? The same is true of all professions. A good physician helps you get well, while a poor one just drains your money or even causes problems. A competent mechanic makes your car run properly, an incompetent one doesn't.

The point is that astrology is a viable science that can be of value in your life. It merits your open-minded consideration.

If this interests you, you have two options. Either have a professional astrologer prepare your natal chart and interpret it for you, or do it yourself. To do it yourself, purchase a beginning astrology book and read it. You should be able to learn enough to enable you to build some of your bridges. Either way is relatively inexpensive.

Astrology does not have all the answers and is not a cure-all. It is just one of many tools available for you to use in order to better orchestrate the direction of your life. It is not fatalistic. In all cases, astrology presents your options. The choice you make is always up to you alone. You alone are the captain of your ship. Astrology merely provides a more complete map for you to set sail with.

Here is a personal story to illustrate one of the many kinds of useful information you can glean from your natal astrology chart.

I was a third level manager in IBM. I had never particularly wanted to be an executive. It just happened. I needed a job, and IBM had an opening and hired me. I was competent and worked hard, and the promotions kept coming along until I had moved up into what many people would regard as a plush position. But I was not happy.

Partly as a lark, and partly to give me an outlet for my pent-up frustrations, I studied astrology at night under the instruction of a professional astrologer. I took up astrology as an avocation.

Of course I studied my own natal astrology chart in

great detail. In relation to occupation, my chart revealed the following:

1. I did have some management and business ability, but it was far from being my strongest ability. Hence, I could do it, but I would not find it especially fulfilling.

2. I had two extremely strong abilities. One was as a communicator, especially as a writer. This confirmed what I had always felt but had never pursued in a disciplined way.

3. The other was the ability to be a hypnotherapist. This took me completely by surprise because I had never once given hypnosis a passing thought.

Armed with this information, I quit my job with IBM, studied and became a certified hypnotherapist, and started writing books, two of which deal with hypnosis. Now I am happy and fulfilled.

My natal chart gave me the information and "jump start" that I needed to get going in the right direction.

The same kind of thing can happen for you.

# Chapter 18

# Dreams

*Reach high, for stars lie hidden in your soul.*
*Dream deep, for every dream precedes the goal.*
                                        Pamela Vaull Starr

Everyone, except those who are psychotic, has dreams every night while they sleep.

Hold on now! Don't get excited! You are not psychotic just because you don't recall having dreamed. Most people don't recall their dreams, but they still have them. You have to have them to maintain mental health.

Some years ago a group of normal people were tested. They were wired to an electroencephalograph (EEG), which is a device for detecting and recording brain waves, while they slept. A technician monitored the EEG, and when it indicated the subject was entering a dream cycle, the technician would awaken the subject. Thus, the subject was deprived of dreaming. After a couple days of being deprived of dreams, the subjects became disoriented and confused. After a few more days they became completely psychotic.

Then the subjects were allowed a night of undisturbed sleep so they could dream. After just one normal night of dreaming, these test subjects became completely normal again. (The preceding paragraphs are my synthesis of material from the book, *Dream Power*, by Dr. Ann Faraday, published in 1972 by Coward, McCann and Geoghegan.)

We can infer from these tests that dreams are vitally important to our health. Perhaps one day someone will discover how to make people who really are psychotic start dreaming and thus become cured.

Aside from the health aspect, dreams are also a source of information, a mechanism for solving problems, entertainment, and even prophecy.

Let me digress briefly at this point to tell you a true story about one dream that was a prophecy.

I was twelve years old and was awakened a little after midnight by the sound of my mother crying in the bedroom adjacent to mine.

I heard my father ask, "What is wrong? Are you all right?"

"Virgil and Marie are dead," Mother sobbed. Virgil was my mother's brother and Marie was his wife.

"You just had a bad dream, but it is not true," Dad answered.

"Yes, it was a dream, but it is true," Mother insisted. "Pa will be here at daybreak to tell us about it. I saw it all and it is true." Pa referred to her father who lived some 35 miles away in Toledo. Neither Grandpa nor us had a telephone so the only way he could contact us was to drive down.

"Hush and go back to sleep," Dad said. "You shouldn't have eaten that snack before bedtime."

Mother didn't go back to sleep. She got up and got dressed to await the arrival of Grandpa.

At six o'clock we heard a car pull up, followed by heavy footsteps on the porch. It was Grandpa. He told us that Uncle Virgil and Aunt Marie were killed a little after midnight when a train struck their car as they returned home from a dance. Another couple in the car with them was also killed.

Dreams are powerful, and there is still a lot we don't know about them, but we do know they are another tool available to you for helping you build bridges to tomorrow. Of course, you must first learn how to remember dreams in order to reap this benefit.

Learning to remember dreams is fairly simple, but it does require persistence. To remember dreams, and understand them, follow these steps:

1. Put paper and pencil near your bed so you can record your dreams when you awaken. Or, if you prefer, have a tape recorder at hand. It is very important that you record your dreams immediately upon awakening, even if it is two o'clock in the morning. If you wait until some later time to record them, it is likely you will have forgotten parts or all of the dreams.

2. When you settle into bed for the night, take a few moments to get comfortable. Close your eyes. Take a couple deep breaths.

3. Then mentally say to yourself, "Tonight I am going to dream and I will remember my dreams completely when I awaken and I will understand the meaning of my dreams." Then go to sleep.

4. When you awaken, record everything you recall. If the meaning doesn't immediately come to you, relax a moment and mentally ask, "What is the meaning of this dream?" You may get an awareness right then or it may come later.

The preceding four steps may work perfectly the first time you try them. Or, you may not get results for several days or even weeks. Don't despair. Hang tough. Keep at it every night. Be persistent, and you will succeed. What you are doing is programming your mind to give you recollection and interpretation of your dreams. For years, your mind has not been accustomed to giving you those things, so the reprogramming may take some practice.

A typical scenario might go like this:

1. The first night you recall fragments of a dream, and that is all.

2. After several nights more, you recall a complete dream.

3. A few nights later, you recall the dream and have an awareness of its meaning.

4. Then you start remembering multiple dreams and their meanings.

Often I don't get the meaning of my dreams until sometime after I awaken. I will awaken and recall the dream, but get no interpretation. So I mentally ask, "What does this dream mean?" Then I go on about my daily routine. I've had the complete interpretation flash into my mind later when shaving, driving, shopping, or some other activity.

Occasionally, I won't recall the dream until some time later. One such occasion was interesting. I awakened with no recollection, so I just went about getting washed, shaved, and dressed. I sat down to put on my shoes. As I bent over to pick up a shoe, a "living color" movie of my dream flashed on the floor. It was a very entertaining movie. My wife was sitting up in bed talking to me at the time. Evidently I must have become transfixed by the movie because I could hear her shouting at me from somewhere on the periphery of my awareness, "Bill! What's wrong? What are you looking at? Are you all right?"

When my dream movie was over, which probably lasted only a minute or so but conveyed enough information for me to dwell on for several hours later, I told my wife what had happened.

She thought I was daft.

Once you get to the point where you can regularly recall your dreams and understand them, you are ready to start using your dreams to solve problems.

To solve problems in your dreams, do the following:

1. Put your pencil and paper, or tape recorder, near your bed.

2. Get comfortable in bed, as instructed before.

3. Mentally say, "Tonight, I want a dream that will provide me information that will enable me to solve my problem. The problem is . . . (briefly state the problem)." Then go to sleep.

4. When you awaken, record your dream or dreams. Ask for the interpretation if you didn't receive it automatically. Your solution, or information leading to the solution, will be there.

Enjoy your dreams and use them. They are a powerful channel for information from Higher Mind to you. You can get information from your dreams to help you with your bridge-building. With practice, you can also program your dreams to build your bridges for you.

Start playing around with your dreams. At the very least you will have a good time. At the most, you will develop a powerful tool to help you program your tomorrows.

There is a saying that the future belongs to those who believe in the beauty of their dreams.

# Chapter 19

# Chronology of a Bridge

*Even the woodpecker owes his success to the fact that he uses his head and keeps pecking away until he finishes the job he starts.*
Coleman Cox

In this chapter I will show you in detail how I constructed two bridges to tomorrow.

The first one was a long, complex one that took many years to complete before I reached the other side of the bridge to where I wanted to be.

You will no doubt have at least one, and probably several, of these complex type bridges in your life.

The second bridge was simple, and it took me quickly to where I wanted to be. You will have many bridges like this in your life.

You will also have many bridges that fall somewhere in between the complex and the simple examples I give here.

## *A Complex Bridge*

Whether I am giving autographs, a lecture, or one-on-one counseling, I am invariably asked, "How does one become a successful author?" So I tell the story of how I did it in hopes that it will help the would-be author to chart his/her course to successful authorship. In a larger sense, the things I learned in my pursuit of becoming a successful author also apply to becoming a success in any pursuit. Here is how I built my bridge to become a successful author.

As far back as I can recall, when I was somewhere in grade school, I knew there were two things I wanted to do when I grew up: one, grow a mustache, and two, become a writer.

I stopped shaving my upper lip when I graduated from high school in 1947. Within a couple of weeks I had a very nice mustache.

Becoming a writer took a little longer.

My first free-lance book was a non-fiction work titled *Daydream Your Way to Success,* that I wrote in 1985; it was published in October 1986 by Llewellyn Publications. The book was retitled *Hypnosis* on the second printing in 1987. I was an overnight success, after 39 years of preparation and bridge-building.

My journey from novice in 1947 to published author in 1986 was like taking a trip from New York to Paris by traveling south to the Strait of Magellan, then northwest to Tahiti in the South Pacific for a stopover; then further west for stopovers in Bangkok, New Delhi, and Alexandria. At any given point it seemed unlikely that Paris was the destination.

But with all the detours and delays, one thing never changed. That was my dream of becoming a writer. And along the way I learned some things about becoming a professional writer.

Having a dream is absolutely essential, but it is nothing except fantasy unless you work the dream and make it become reality.

It is like owning a piece of land under which lies a fabulously rich gold mine. Having the land is essential to gaining the wealth it contains, but unless you work the land to extract the gold you will not become wealthy. Dreaming of the gold that is underground is not enough. You must work to extract it.

So how do you work the dream of becoming a writer to make it become reality?

Let me tell you about my journey which began shortly after I got my mustache.

I bought my first typewriter, a Smith-Corona portable. I took stock of my assets: I was a high school graduate and could read and write; I was an excellent typist; I knew how to use a dictionary; I was a voracious reader. Conclusion: I was a writer.

So I wrote. And wrote. And wrote some more. For years. Only no one would buy what I wrote. I collected enough rejection slips to provide fuel for a very large bonfire. By 1960, the message penetrated my thick skull . . . I must not be doing something right.

A *Writer's Digest* magazine caught my eye at the newsstand, and I bought it. Inside there was an ad for a writing course that *Writer's Digest* offered. As I recall, the cost was $50 for fourteen correspondence lessons.

At the time, I was an electronics technician for IBM earning a little over $100 a week. (I learned the skill in the Air Force where I had spent six years.) I was married and had three children. Fifty dollars was a lot of money to me, and I knew I would incur my wife's wrath if I spent money on "such foolishness."

I did it anyway. I figured if I wasn't willing to invest in myself, I couldn't expect editors to invest in me. My first lesson arrived in May, 1960.

The wrath did come, but so did *Writer's Digest's* fiction writing course. That course really opened my eyes. Everything a writer can do wrong, I had been doing zealously. Only by accident had I also been doing a couple things right. It was my moment of truth . . . writing was a skill that needed to be learned. Being literate did not automatically make one a writer.

The improvement in my writing was dramatic. I sold five short stories to minor magazines between September, 1962, and January, 1967. Not exactly a "barn burner" record, is it? But successes, none the less. I was writing and getting paid (not much) for it. Three of those stories were juveniles which I literally took from my own children's antics. The other two were for a woman's magazine (which went defunct right after my second story was published) that I patterned from my own family life.

In 1962 something else was happening. The computer boom had started and I was right in the middle of it at IBM. I had the computer training, and I could also write. IBM asked me to write badly needed technical manuals for their rapidly expanding data processing line.

I thought I had died and gone to heaven. Here I was writing full-time and getting paid for it. I loved the work and it loved me. Every time I turned around I was getting a raise and a promotion. IBM had two excellent professional editors, and I learned a great deal from them. I got paid to hone my writing skills. I couldn't believe it. I had to pinch myself daily to see if I was really not dreaming it all.

While technical writing paid the bills and honed my skills, it still wasn't the dream I had had since childhood.

I wanted to be a real writer. One who creates. One who free-lances. One who writes million-seller books and gives autographs. One who sells to national magazines. I wanted to write for me, not for some corporation.

So I bought a new IBM Selectric® typewriter at a discount through payroll deductions and set about to write great novels and stories at night and on weekends, while supporting myself as a technical writer.

I wrote. And wrote. And wrote some more. For years. Only no one would buy what I wrote. I quickly collected enough rejection slips for another bonfire.

What was I doing wrong? Before I could settle on an answer, IBM promoted me to Technical Publications Manager and transferred me to Boulder, Colorado to create and manage a new publications department.

I was so busy growing from a department of five to one of forty-seven people over the next six years that I didn't write a word, although I kept my dream alive in my mind.

In October, 1973, I faced the truth. I was successful in corporate management, but I wasn't happy. I never did like it. It was the money and nothing else that had captured me. I still wanted to be a real writer. After eighteen years with IBM, I quit. Just like that. My wife had a fit.

Before I could warm up the keys on my Selectric, several bizarre personal experiences took me off in a different direction. Those experiences are not germane to this article, so I'll spare you the details. Suffice it to say that I became a qualified professional hypnotherapist and a qualified astrologer. For the next four years I partially supported my family as a hypnotherapist and astrologer, which eased the drain on our savings. I continue to practice these skills to this day.

My unfulfilled dream kept haunting me. I needed to write, and I also needed to support my family. The solution came to me on New Year's Day, 1977. Why not return to technical writing? I was good at that, and I now realized that it was real writing, even though my byline didn't appear on any of the dozens of technical manuals I had written. And I also vowed to develop a plan to become a good, successful free-lance writer. This time I made a commitment to myself to stop dallying. I was determined to be an author.

Sometimes I worked directly for a company, and sometimes I worked on a contract basis, but I kept busy writing technical material for industry.

In the meantime, I analyzed my past successes and non-successes (I don't ever use the word failure in connection with myself). In October 1983 I cried, "Eureka!" Now I understood. When I wrote about things from my own experience, I succeeded. When I tried to write the great American novel and other similar works I fell flat, because I was writing from the vantage point of ignorance. This "new" revelation was something the *Writer's Digest* writing course had taught me years earlier, and I had ignored it.

Now was commitment time. I did four things to cement my commitment.

1. I began reading *Writer's Digest* magazine every month. I had been a hit and miss reader previously.

2. I purchased *Writer's Market* and studied it.

3. I joined The National Writers Club as an associate member where I could get professional guidance. I believe some sort of professional affiliation tends to spur one on when it would be easier to quit.

4. I purchased a computer system with word processing capabilities to ease the mechanical drudgery of writing, revising, and formatting. I wanted to spend the maximum amount of time creating rather than retyping. My system consists of: Commodore 64 computer; Commodore 13" color monitor; two Commodore disk drives; a Gemini 10X dot matrix printer; a Paperclip-64 word processing program. Total cost was about $1100. I later added an Epson DX10 daisy wheel letter quality printer for less than $400.

I was in business for real. Now I had to write. My wife would hand me my head if I didn't write after spending that much money.

So I wrote a non-fiction book about a subject I knew quite well: *Hypnosis*. Mr. Carl Llewellyn Weschcke, president of Llewellyn Publications, liked the manuscript and gave me a royalty contract.

I quickly wrote an article about astrology (another subject about which I know something) and *Horoscope Guide* magazine bought it and published it.

Other articles and five more books quickly followed over the next several years. The National Writers Club upgraded my membership to "Professional Member."

I began to get offers to give lectures and workshops based on my books, which I eagerly accepted.

There is absolutely no doubt in my mind that I am now a bona fide, real, professional writer. I built and crossed my bridge. It is a nice, quiet, comfortable feeling. To cross that bridge, I had to learn seven lessons:

1. Have a dream.

2. Invest in myself.

3. Learn the skills of writing.

4. Make a commitment.

5. Write about those things I know something about—things from my own experience.

6. Never give up. Persevere.

7. Work That Dream.

I still continue to support myself with contract technical writing. I will do so until I have sufficient royalty money and other writing monies coming in to make me comfortable. In the meantime, I will write, and write, and continue to write. But now, I will also sell and be published.

P.S. I still have my mustache.

### *A Simple Bridge*

Some years ago my work took me to a mid-sized city in upstate New York, and I resided in a small town adjacent to that city. We had lived there several years when general election time rolled around, and my wife and I went to the polling place to register since we had not been previously registered in New York state.

My wife is Chinese, and she was the only non-Caucasian living in the small town.

She preceded me in the registration line. When her turn came, they refused to let her register because she didn't bring her birth certificate with her. (No one else had been asked to show a birth certificate.)

I recognized immediately that they were acting solely on blind prejudice, but I controlled my rising temper.

"She is a citizen, born in New Orleans," I reasoned as calmly as I could, "and we have lived here in town several years. You know that."

"I have the legal right to demand a birth certificate!" the man in charge said defiantly.

"We will be back," I said.

We drove home, got my wife's birth certificate and returned to get back in the registration line five minutes before registration ended.

When her turn came again, the five members of the registration board passed my wife's birth certificate around among them. Then they held a whispering huddle.

The board leader said, "Sorry. This is not enough. We need to see a high school diploma."

Now I was really angry, and I shed my Mr. Nice Guy demeanor.

"No!" I snapped. "You do not have to see her diploma. That is not a legal requirement to register to vote and you know it!"

"Well, we are not going to register her!" the man snapped back.

My wife was in tears.

"Don't waste tears over these five poor excuses for humanity," I said. "They are going to be the ones to shed tears before I am through with them!"

We left the place with neither of us registered, and the registration was now legally closed. I was already building my bridge in my mind. I knew who was in back of us in line both times and were witnesses. I intended to get us both registered, get an official apology, and get the entire registration board reprimanded. That was my bridge.

I knew the name of a local politician who was reputed to be both honest and powerful. I phoned an attorney friend who gave me the politician's address, and I drove there. Within fifteen minutes after being denied registration I was in the politician's living room talking to him.

The politician was as angry as I over what had happened. He promised to get back with me the next day.

Result: He had the five people severely reprimanded, I got an official apology, and most importantly, he told us to show up and vote on election day because he made the board register us without our having to come back again.

That was a bridge I constructed in seconds and crossed successfully in a very short time.

The aftermath is sort of funny. When we went in to vote, the same five people were on the election board. When it was our turn, they were all smiles.

"Nice to see you, Mrs. Hewitt and Mr. Hewitt." They acted like long-lost cousins. They couldn't have been more solicitous.

And from that point on, everyone in town knew us and addressed us by name. People became friendly and made deliberate attempts to make small talk when they encountered us on the street or in a store.

My bridges had been built on my determination and on my refusal to ever allow anyone or anything to intimidate me. I have always believed that if you are right and refuse to give up, nothing can defeat you.

I hope that sharing these two experiences with you helps you gain an even clearer picture of what building bridges to tomorrow is all about.

Basically it amounts to this: You have a goal you want to achieve, and you marshal all the personal traits, information, and help you need to achieve the goal, while pursuing the goal with determination until you achieve it.

The only way you can fail is if:

1. You give up.

2. You do not develop and use the personal traits necessary.

3. You do not attain the necessary information.

4. You do not enlist the necessary help.

If you notice in my first bridge example, I did not do a good job on items 2, 3, and 4 for a long time, and I did not succeed for a long time. When I finally got myself trained and properly tended to items 2, 3, and 4, I achieved success quickly. Item 1 is the only thing I did right for a long time, but that was enough to keep me going until I realized what else needed to be done.

In my second bridge example I did all four things right from the start and I achieved immediate success.

To paraphrase something Galileo said centuries ago: You cannot teach people anything. You can only help them find it within themselves.

This book is to help you find it within yourself, to build your bridges for successful tomorrows.

# Chapter 20

# Is There a Ninny in Your Life?

*A great many people think they are thinking when they are merely rearranging their prejudices.*

William James

What is a ninny? The dictionary defines ninny as: a fool; simpleton. That is not the meaning of ninny in this chapter. In this chapter I will use Hewitt's definition of ninny, which is:

A person who is mentally and physically able to shoulder responsibility but who deliberately shirks every bit of responsibility he/she possibly can by getting someone else to do it for him/her. Ninnies are leeches on society in general, and on any specific person they can sucker into carrying their load. Being a ninny is not a desirable trait.

Shortly I will give some specific examples of ninnies I have observed to give you a clearer picture of what one is. I will discuss one group of ninnies and a number of individual ninnies.

If you are reading this book, the chances are very high that you are not a ninny, because this book is for people who are looking to exercise their responsibilities in such a way as to improve their life. Ninnies rarely consider self-improvement; they think they don't need it. After all, they are doing quite nicely in life by letting someone else do everything for them.

There is a chance, however, that there is a ninny in your life who is depleting some of the quality of your life. If so, you need to do something about it in order to have a happier, more successful life for yourself.

To enlarge on my definition of ninny: Ninnies usually are quite lazy (but not always). They are frequently cowards. They are almost never courageous or creative. They usually like the "status quo"; little or no change from whatever is important to them. They are almost always insensitive to the rights of others, thus they are selfish and self-centered. "I" tends to be a word they use a lot.

A ninny can be a man or a woman of any age from puberty on. Below puberty, children are struggling for identity, and I would not want to brand them as ninnies because of a behavior that they are confused by themselves.

As a group, the Ku Klux Klan (and similar white supremacist groups) represents the largest concentration of ninnies that I can think of. They dress in sheets and hoods for fear of recognition, and do their dirty work mostly under cover of night, out of personal fear. They travel in well-armed groups so they can attack an individual unarmed negro, Jew, or other person who they fear. They do everything in their power to deprive others of their rights because they have made up their mind that they cannot tolerate any change from "status quo." They are cowards of the first order, and the most creative thing they know how to do is burn crosses.

The KKK cannot survive without support from non-KKK members. Family and friends of KKK members support them emotionally and financially. Even if you do nothing to be nonsupportive, you are giving support by acquiescence. Judges, lawyers, the government, and individual citizens support the KKK either directly or by doing nothing. Remember, all it takes for evil to exist is for good people to do nothing.

I started out with the illustration of the KKK to drive home the point that ninnies are a drag—a leech—on everyone they can sink their tentacles into. I'll now give you some examples of the individual ninnies you are most likely to encounter in your personal, everyday life.

**Scenario #1:** You are busy preparing a nice Sunday dinner for you and your husband. He is sitting in the family room watching the "big game." Outside the snow has been falling since yesterday afternoon and about a foot of snow has accumulated in the driveway. He has found excuses to not shovel the driveway or sidewalk yesterday and today. His back is acting up on him again (it only acts up when there is work to be done). Besides, it is too cold to be out (it is always "too cold" because he is sensitive to cold except when there is a football game to attend).

At that moment, an electrical fuse blows in the house. He quickly runs and gets the small battery operated television. "Lucky it happened during a commercial," he says. Then he calls up to you, "You'd better get

the fuse changed so you can fix dinner! Besides the bat-
teries in this television will only last a couple hours."

"My hands are in water. I am washing the lettuce
for salad," you respond. "Please change the fuse. It is
down by you in the utility room. I can't finish baking
the chicken."

Silence. He suddenly has gotten selective hearing
and doesn't hear you. He can hear the game quite
well, though.

You call down again, shouting loud enough to be
heard four houses away. Still silence. He does not
respond. So you plod down to the utility room. There are
no spare fuses.

You go to where he is sitting. "We are out of fuses.
Please run to the hardware store and get some."

"You can go," he says without lifting his eyes from
the television.

"I am busy preparing dinner. Besides the driveway
isn't clear, and I don't drive well in snow."

"Just shovel enough to get the car out," he says.
"You will do all right. You only have to drive a mile to
the hardware store."

Now your voice goes up 10 decibels, "I am not
going to get the fuse! I am busting my hump cooking! If
you don't get the fuse, we don't eat! You can help around
here once in a while!"

"Then put a penny in the fuse box!" he shouts back.
"That will work! Now let me watch my game in peace!"

This guy is a classic ninny. He gets away with it
because you, and probably others, let him get away with
it. And in so doing, you diminish your happiness and
success. After a few more scenarios, we'll discuss some
bridges you may want to build to prevent ninnies from
draining your chances for success and happiness.

**Scenario #2:** The wife beater. These ninnies rank right up there with the Ku Klux Klan. They are an intolerable scourge. They get away with it because the wife, society, and the justice system tolerate them. By doing nothing, we sanction their unacceptable behavior.

No one has the right to do physical harm to another person except in self-defense or in defense of another person. Even if your husband catches you kissing the postman, he does not have the right to physically harm you in any manner whatsoever. He has the right to separate from you or divorce you, but not to physically harm you.

**Scenario #3:** Child abuser. Men and women who do this are NINNIES with capital letters. Absolutely no excuses for this behavior—ever!

**Scenario #4:** Here is a couple I know. He is physically healthy and has a driver's license. However, when they go anywhere together he refuses to drive; it makes him nervous or his back aches. When they stop for gasoline he won't even get out and pump it; she has to do it. At home when he wants a beer, he hollers for her to get it for him even though the refrigerator is within a few steps from him and she is in another part of the house.

On a recent motor trip that was a 10-hour drive, the wife asked him to relieve her at the wheel after five hours because she was getting groggy. He said, "Just continue to drive to the next place where we can get some coffee. Coffee will perk you up and you will be able to continue."

She refused to continue because she was afraid of having an accident. "Women!" he said in disgust. He took over driving for fifteen minutes, whereupon there was a truck stop. He stopped at the truck stop where they both had a cup of coffee. Then he got back into the passenger seat. "Your turn to drive," he said as he closed his eyes to rest.

When they go on vacation he refuses to take part in any of the planning, refuses to pack his own things, will not carry the suitcases, and expects her to do the airport check-in. When they reach their destination, guess who then gripes because something he wanted wasn't packed, and he doesn't like the lodging she picked, etc. You are right—the big Ninny!

**Scenario #5:** I was in the Air Force for six years and met at least one of every kind of human being there is. The military is a great melting pot of humanity. There is one particular ninny who stands out in my memory. I'll call him "the conscientious objector."

I'm not talking about the legitimate conscientious objectors. I knew quite a few of these also. They all were honest, courageous men whose sincere religious beliefs prevented them from carrying a gun or killing people for any reason. When they enlisted they declared themselves to be conscientious objectors up front. They willingly did whatever they could to serve their country without killing. Many were killed in the line of duty as medics and ambulance drivers. Brave men, all.

The one I am talking about I'll call Harley. I knew Harley for several years before the Korean War erupted. Harley was a drinker, gambler, and womanizer. He had never been inside a church. His favorite pastime was brawling in a barroom. None of the guys liked Harley very much because he was extremely self-centered. His lifestyle was his business; I have no quarrel with that.

Then war broke out. The first contingency from our Air Base was shipped to Korea, and we knew there would be more to follow.

The Sunday after the first overseas shipment to Korea, Harley went to church. In fact he spent all of his off duty time at the chapel. He stopped his carousing, and became the chaplain's regular little helper. He carried a large bible with him every place, including to the mess hall to eat, so everyone could see how religious he was.

Shortly, Harley's name appeared on the roster for shipment to Korea. He immediately declared himself to be a conscientious objector and asked to be taken off the roster.

The squadron commander refused to remove Harley from the roster. "You are a motor pool mechanic," the Colonel had said. "That isn't a combat position."

Harley countered, "But I will be in a war zone and might be forced to kill someone. Anyway, I would be repairing vehicles that would be used in war, and that is against my religious beliefs." He then asked to be given an honorable discharge.

The Colonel wasn't fooled by Harley. He told Harley, "No discharge and no exemption from going to Korea."

Harley walked out of the Colonel's office and disappeared—went AWOL. I don't know if they ever did find him.

Harley was a ninny!

**Scenario #6:** A friend had an adult daughter who wouldn't work. There was nothing wrong with her except laziness.

She slept until noon, stuffed herself with any food she could find that didn't require cooking (such as bread and peanut butter), primped with her face and hair for an hour, and then disappeared to some friend's house until dinner time. She rarely missed dinner, and then she disappeared again with friends until the wee hours of the next morning. Of course, she would not help her mother with after dinner clean up. This was her daily ritual. She was a ninny.

Both parents had tried talking with her, reasoning with her, and even almost pleading—all to no avail.

Exasperated, my friend finally issued an ultimatum, "Today you will go out and get a job or you no longer have a place to live here." He asked for the house key back and handed her the want ads from the newspaper.

She left the house pouting. At dinner time she returned and rang the doorbell. My friend answered the door.

"No one would give me a job," she said. "I'll try again tomorrow." She tried to enter the house, but her father blocked her way.

"No," her father said. "You are not welcome here until you have a job." He shut the door in her face. He knew she was lying—that she hadn't even attempted to look for a job.

An hour and a half later the doorbell rang again. It was the daughter, and she had a grin on her face. "I got a job as a waitress starting tomorrow at the Village Inn," she announced. The restaurant was only two miles away.

Once she started to work, she liked it. She discovered that work wasn't an ordeal at all. She also liked having money and the independence that money gave her. She quickly earned a promotion to supervisor on the day shift.

Several years later she decided she wanted more out of life, so she put herself through a two-year nursing school. Today she is a registered nurse, working harder than she had ever dreamed possible, and loving it.

Some ninnies can be rehabilitated. She is no longer a ninny.

**Scenario #7:** Another friend had a similar situation with his adult son as the one described in scenario #6. The son was about as lazy as a person could get. He wouldn't work, period. He wouldn't even keep himself clean. He stunk from body odor. His breath would wilt flowers. Sleep, television, and eat (only if someone prepared the food) were all he would engage in. Left alone, he would not even fix a peanut butter sandwich; he would go hungry or just drink water until his mother fixed him something.

Both parents tried everything they could, including professional counseling, but nothing worked. He got verbally abusive with the parents and the counselor. He got physically abusive at home, throwing objects at his parents or deliberately breaking things.

After a year of counseling with absolutely no progress or change, the parents had had it. Their nerves were shot. They realized their own lives were being wasted on a ninny. They dropped the counselor. They located a furnished apartment, paid one month's rent on it, and moved their son in. They took him on a grocery shopping trip so he would know how.

"You are on your own now," they told him. "No more help from us." And they stuck to it.

The son survived and is still surviving on his own. He knows exactly what the minimum is that he needs to do to just skim by, and that is all he does. He managed to get himself put on welfare so he had food stamps and some money. He finds other people to poach off. When people find out he is a free loader they drop him, but he quickly finds others.

He still is unclean most of the time, although he has improved a little in this area. He buys only prepared food that requires no cooking. The most he will cook is to warm a can of soup.

He is still a professional ninny, and I think he always will be. Ninnies are very difficult, and in many cases nearly impossible, to rehabilitate.

But at least the parents had the guts to divorce their son and get on with their own lives in peace and happiness.

**Scenario #8:** Then there is the neighbor who knocks at your door holding her infant. "Would you watch my baby for just a few minutes. I have a quick errand to run. I will be back shortly."

You take the baby. You were just about to leave to do your grocery shopping, but a few minutes delay won't hurt.

An hour passes and the baby is fussy and hungry. The mother didn't leave a bottle or any food.

Two hours. The baby is soaked and smelly and has been screaming for the past thirty minutes.

Three hours. The baby won't shut up, and you are weary trying to soothe the child. You phone to see if the mother has returned. No answer.

Another thirty minutes pass, and you see the mother drive into her driveway. She begins unloading her groceries and other packages from a department store. This really burns you up. Your own shopping trip won't get done now because your neighbor has just taken advantage of your good nature.

Another thirty minutes and she still hasn't come for her child. Angry, you carry the child to her house and pound on the door. When the door opens you can hear a soap opera on the television.

The woman takes the screaming baby. "Is mommy's baby hungry?" she says, taking the baby from your arms and closing the door in your face.

Not even a "thank you."

Every neighborhood has at least one of this specie of ninny.

I've given eight scenarios (nine counting the KKK) to illustrate what a ninny is. There are hundreds of other varieties of ninny, but I believe you have enough information to recognize them for what they are.

The reason I am spending so much time on ninnies is because they can be a significant deterrent to your happiness and success if you are involved with them. Unfortunately, there are a great number of ninnies in our society so your chances are high of being involved with at least one of them at some time in your life.

Ninnies rob enjoyment and success from others and from themselves.

If you recognize yourself as being a ninny and if you want success and happiness, you are going to have to make a significant attitude adjustment and build some bridges to greater sensitivity, greater respect for others and to yourself, and a lot of other bridges. It can be done if you really want it. The other chapters in this book will show you many ways to make the necessary changes by building bridges.

If you encounter ninnies in your life, you are going to have to stop them from using you if you want to achieve your own personal development. You are going to have to build bridges that take you away from their tentacles.

Let's reexamine our nine scenarios and see what your options might be in dealing with the situation.

The Ku Klux Klan: If your husband, a relative, or close friend is a KKK member (or a member of any similar hate group) you might first try to talk to them heart to heart to get them to quit. If this doesn't work, which it most likely won't, then I see no options except divorce or separating yourself completely from them. If I were a woman married to a KKK member, I would get a divorce and would let the whole world know why. This is a tough situation, and you must decide what is best for you.

Recently, voters in one state elected the ex-Grand Dragon of the Ku Klux Klan to the state legislature. They apparently didn't realize how that action demeaned them and the whole state. I wouldn't want to have to look at myself in the mirror every day mindful I had knowingly voted for someone who supports murdering, brutalizing, and intimidating various minority groups as a matter of routine. That same ex-KKK member ran for governor, intent on grooming himself for a presidential bid. However, the voters now realized their previous mistake, and the man was resoundingly defeated, crushing any presidential aspirations. I hope we never vote a ninny into the White House!

If you are not willing to dump these ninnies, then you may as well remain loyal to your KKK friends, because you have already achieved as much in life as you are likely to.

You don't have to put up with these people and their unwelcome behavior. Here is how I would handle these situations:

In Scenario #1, the lazy, selfish, responsibility shirking spouse. First try to talk with him (or her) in a rational, mature manner. The chances are high that it will fall on deaf ears, but you owe it to both of you to try this first.

Absolutely do not bow to his (or her) unreasonableness. In this scenario, don't prepare him anything to eat. Fix yourself something (if only a peanut butter sandwich); let him go hungry. If the blown fuse affects your heating system, just bundle up and tough it out. He will get cold and hungry and will eventually get off his duff and do something constructive about it. You must take a hard line and stick to it. If everything you try does not work, you will probably need to separate or divorce unless you are willing to spend the rest of your life as a slave to a ninny.

In Scenario #2, the wife beater. Get a restraining order. Boot the ninny out. Allow the ninny to return *only* after he successfully completes a professional counseling and rehabilitation program. Don't fool around with this ninny. You must take a hard stand immediately and stick to it.

In Scenario #3, the child abuser. Same as #2 above. Don't fool around. Take legal action.

In Scenario #4, a parasite spouse. Take action similar to scenario #1. Refuse to give in. Of course, try a heart-to-heart talk first. The ninny may be such a dolt that he is unaware of his unreasonable actions.

In Scenario #5, you probably need to sever all relationships with this kind of ninny.

Scenario #6 illustrates that some ninnies can be rehabilitated if you take a hard line with them and stick to it.

In Scenario #7, some ninnies are not rehabilitatible, but you must take a hard line for your own happiness and success.

In Scenario #8, the imposing neighbor. The first time something like this happens, it is not your fault. You are trying to be a helpful neighbor. However, if you allow this person to misuse you again, then that *is* your fault. You must have the guts to say "NO" loud and clear. When you do, they will quickly shift their energies to searching for someone else to misuse.

## *Summary*

You need to become sensitive to the games ninnies play, and not allow yourself to be a participant. You need to build bridges to shore up your own willpower to say "NO," to take a hard line, to ensure your rights, and to ensure your own happiness and success.

Dealing with ninnies is not always easy or pleasant, but you must build those bridges to isolate them from interfering with your rights if you want to achieve maximum happiness and success in your life.

Parasites must have someone to feed on for them to survive in a "ninny" mode of living. If they have no feeding ground, they must change to becoming a non-ninny in order to survive.

Don't allow yourself to be their feeding ground! Build the proper bridges!.

# Chapter 21

# **Compromise**

*This above all; to thine own self be true,*
*And it must follow, as the night the day,*
*Thou canst not then be false to any man.*
                                    William Shakespeare

All evil has its birth in compromise.

This does not mean that all compromise is evil. On the contrary, most compromise is a necessary part of life. Union and management negotiate, and each side compromises their positions in order to reach a workable, fair settlement for all concerned. The teenager wants to stay out until 2 a.m. The parents want to impose a 9 p.m. curfew. They talk it over and compromise on an 11 p.m. curfew. You want a new Ferrari automobile, but your finances would be destroyed if you bought one, so you compromise on a less expensive car. Compromise is a necessary part of everyone's life at one time or another.

Compromise gives birth to evil and to problems when you compromise your integrity, honesty, value system, loyalty, self-esteem, reputation, judgment, or trust; usually for some sort of perceived personal gain. Most often the evil that is born from this sort of compromise is GREED, which is probably the most destructive of all traits.

I bring this subject up because it is vitally important in how you build your bridges in your quest for success and happiness. The moment you build a bridge flawed with personal compromise of your character in order to achieve something, you set the stage for problems (usually major ones) that will plague you and may even bring about your downfall.

Let me cite several examples to make the point.

**Example #1:** Richard Nixon compromised his integrity and the trust of the Presidency itself in the Watergate scandal. He also lied blatantly. He apparently wanted to perpetuate his delusion of self-righteousness, power, and supremacy. The evil he created in this compromise brought about his downfall and earned him a place in history as a dishonest, power-crazed president. He also shook the very foundations of our government and created distrust in the presidency itself. He achieved exactly the opposite of what he hoped to by making this ill-fated compromise.

Would you be willing to compromise yourself knowing that you could potentially be shamed in front of the entire world? It isn't worth the risk, is it?

**Example #2:** The Savings and Loan scandal of the late 1980s and early 1990s resulted from many people compromising their judgment and integrity. This compromise gave birth to greed. Now the entire country must pay for it.

Innocent people must pay the price for a few greedy people who willingly compromised their judgment and integrity for "easy money" and favors.

It is quite likely the guilty parties will never be able to fully rectify this grave error for themselves, and certainly not for others. The final outcome is not known at this writing and probably won't be known for many years. This is a colossal disaster.

One thing is clear: the perpetrators of this scandal have exposed themselves as being greedy, common thieves. Their facade of respectability has been stripped away forever. Think of the huge negative karma they created for themselves.

Would you want to be in their shoes? Anytime you compromise yourself, you create the very real possibility that you could end up in an equally unpleasant situation.

**Example #3:** You are a political novice running for your first political office: state representative. You are scrambling to get money and support so you can wage a successful campaign. A man who you know by reputation, Mr. Big, a powerful wheeler-dealer, contacts you. He is willing to pull strings, open doors, and contribute money (some of it "under the table") to ensure your election. All he wants in return is one small favor. When you get elected he wants you to introduce a water rights bill that he will furnish. You say okay, and you are elected. You introduce his bill, which you recognize as greatly beneficial to Mr. Big but detrimental to small farmers. The bill passes and becomes law.

A few years later you have the opportunity to run for the United States Congress. Mr. Big again steps forward to help, no strings attached. You let him help and you get elected. Then comes the payoff. He wants a never ending string of favors, most of which are unethical and even shady.

You say, "No."

He reminds you that he now owns you. You took "under the table" money from him on several occasions and you pushed through his tainted water legislation a few years back. "If I let the truth leak out," he threatens, "you are all washed up politically and might even go to jail."

You have been had because you compromised your integrity. You are no longer in control of your own destiny. Someone else owns you and controls you.

This may be the single biggest detriment when you compromise yourself. You turn control of your life over to someone else, and you become a puppet dancing on a string to someone else's tune. Not a good deal at all, is it?

I used this hypothetical political scenario as an example, but the results are the same anytime you compromise yourself in any situation: You turn part of your life over to someone else. This is a fact, so think about it when you build your bridges. Do you want a bridge that you are proud to cross, or do you want one that someone else helped you build and which you are ashamed to cross?

This book is dedicated to putting you in complete control of your own bridge-building—no compromises!

**Example #4:** You are a teenage girl, and there is tremendous peer pressure put on you to give up your virginity. You had decided you wanted to wait until you got older, met Mr. Right, and got married. But guys will not date you unless you give in to their wants. Other girls tauntingly call you "goody-two-shoes" and other names. Whatever you do is your choice alone, but consider this:

Others want you to give up what is yours for their benefit. Doesn't sound like a fair exchange, does it? You give, and they receive. What is in it for you?

What is in it for you is a bridge to potential problems for you alone, if you compromise your integrity. What kind of problems? Possible pregnancy, and it will be you, not one of them, who is pregnant; possible venereal disease, AIDS, or other infections. Certainly there will be loss of self-esteem. You could gain the reputation of being the town "pin cushion." You get the picture. You are gambling your personal self-worth with zero chance of winning anything. You have better odds in Las Vegas betting on the roulette wheel.

In example #4 I am not talking just about teenage girls and their virginity. I am talking about any person, male or female, at any age, who faces a tough decision about exchanging their personal worth for a chance for a potentially nebulous gain.

When you compromise your integrity, honesty, values, judgment, self-esteem, etc., you automatically build a bridge to problems. The problems are not always insurmountable, but they cannot be erased. All you can do is build other bridges to overcome the problems the best you can and go on to achieve the best life you can.

Anytime you compromise yourself in a manner described in this chapter, you automatically create some sort of bad karma that you must deal with.

Wouldn't it be smarter to build bridges without ever compromising yourself?

# Chapter 22

# Suicide

*To be or not to be, that is the question.*
William Shakespeare

Probably most people, at some time in their lives, have the thought pass through their mind that it would be a relief to die and end all the difficulties of this life.

Fortunately, most people do not give serious consideration to that passing thought. For these people, it was just a thought born out of self-pity, at a moment when the future seemed hopeless.

Like all moments, it passes, and the sun comes out again and the feeling of hopelessness fades into the shadows. Life goes on. Suicide is forgotten because of the realization that it is a permanent solution to a temporary problem. It is like pulling out all of your teeth because one of them hurts. It just doesn't make sense.

Unfortunately, an increasingly large number of people are not able to let the moment pass. They dwell on the moment until it clouds their ability to see the sun. They see no viable future for themselves, so they commit suicide, or attempt to.

Twice in my life (in 1972 and in 1976) I had to deal with suicidal people. This may not make me an expert, but it sure gave me some insights that I would like to pass on to you.

The first time it was a friend. He felt he was a complete failure. His parents, siblings, friends, and wife had made him feel he was grossly inadequate. He felt he was an inadequate parent. He was in his late thirties and felt he had not progressed as much in life as he should have or as much as others felt he should have. These were his perceptions.

I got into the act the day after he had attempted to kill himself. Fortunately, his wife had come home unexpectedly from work and found him. She saved his life.

When I talked to him he said, "I have the right to kill myself if I want to. It is my body and my life."

The defiant way he said it told me that he was still thinking of suicide. I knew I had to do something fast.

"Yes, you do have the right," I said gently. That really set him back. He couldn't believe what I had said.

"You agree with me?"

"I agree that you have the right. But I do *not* agree that you should kill yourself. You are already planning your next suicide attempt, aren't you?"

He was visibly shaken, and he started to cry. "How did you know?"

"How I know isn't important. What is important is that you don't do it. Just because you have the right to do something does not mean that it *is right* to do it."

He stared at me blankly.

I continued. "You also have the right to live, and that is right to do. You have spent nearly forty years exploring your option to die. You have spent no time exploring your option to live. In all fairness to yourself, you should at least fully explore both sides of the issue before making a decision."

Before I left him that day he agreed to explore his option to live before making a final decision, if I would help him. I told him I would talk with him two hours every day for two weeks to help him explore his option to live, if he would allow me to call a physician immediately and get him on a medical therapy program. He said okay.

He is alive today. His children are grown. He is happy and content because he cleared his perspective back in 1972. He learned that other people's opinions of him didn't count. Only his opinion counted. He also learned that what he perceived about himself and others at that time was not accurate. He learned that what he thought was a permanent, insurmountable problem was really a temporary problem, caused mainly by his "fuzzy" thinking.

He had learned to build his bridge of life to tomorrow. The second case, in 1976, was a woman who was a complete stranger. I encountered her when she was actually enroute to kill herself.

She was in her fifties, and the verbal and physical abuse from her husband and adult son that she had endured for years had convinced her that she was worthless. She turned to alcohol to dull the pain. She wanted to die.

I used a similar approach with her as I had done with my friend four years earlier. It worked.

Within two weeks she had seen an attorney and obtained a restraining order against her husband and son and had filed for divorce. She hired a private detective to evict the husband and son. She stopped drinking and got a full time job at a local supermarket.

It has been several years since I last talked to her. At that time she told me that the years since her planned suicide have been the best she has ever known. She was happy. She was glad she explored her option to live and build her bridge of life to tomorrow.

The popular singer/songwriter Billy Joel had attempted suicide twice in his early twenties, because it seemed to him there was no hope for his future.

Fortunately for him and for the world, he did not succeed in killing himself. The rest is history. Billy Joel is now one of the most successful and beloved songwriters and singers of our time.

I heard Billy Joel on a television talk show. He talked about how he loves life and how glad he was that he was a failure at suicide. Just a few days after his second suicide attempt some doors had opened up for him, and he was on his way up the ladder of a successful life.

The message is this:

Explore your option to live. Tomorrow is a better day; you can assure that by building a sturdy bridge of life to tomorrow. If you kill yourself today, you permanently prevent tomorrow from coming; you prevent all the wonderful possibilities for yourself.

My radio is playing while I am writing this chapter. Right now the late Dinah Washington is singing "What A Difference A Day Makes." How apropos!

A day makes all the difference in the world. Tomorrow is only a day away. So build your bridge to tomorrow now. Make it a bridge of life. You will never regret it.

# Chapter 23

# What is Dying?

*Death is not the enemy of life, but its friend, for it is the knowledge that our years are limited which makes them so precious. It is the truth that time is but lent to us which makes us, at our best, look upon our years as a trust handed into our temporary keeping.*

Joshua Loth Liebman

We are all experts at dying. We have done it many times in past lives and will do it again at least once more. Most likely we will do it again many more times. This is because we are eternal beings and we must incarnate a number of times through this earth existence until we learn what it is we need to learn.

Of course, we usually have no recollection of these past death experiences. Using hypnotic regression, I have taken several people through previous death and rebirth sequences. I have also experienced previous death through self-regression. But other than this kind of experience, one usually has no recollection of previous death.

This means that most people view their inevitable death during this lifetime as a "first," and they are often concerned about it. what is it like? When will it come? Will it hurt? What, if anything, happens after death? The questions go on and on.

There are a number of excellent books on the market about this subject, and I do not intend to repeat what has already been written by persons more learned than I on this matter.

However, I do have a few important comments to offer on the subject that I have gotten through my own experiences and meditations.

First, understand this. Only your container, which you call your body, actually dies. Your container is of this earth dimension, composed of materials that have a "shelf life" so to speak, and is therefore destined to terminate at some time.

You, on the other hand, are spiritual and exist in all dimensions, even though you currently have no conscious awareness of the other dimensions. You are eternal. You never die. You never cease to exist. You are pure intelligent energy.

So you, the intelligent energy, temporarily inhabit a container which will one day die. At that time, you will exit the container and exit the current earth cycle you are now experiencing.

When will this happen? If you do not prematurely end your life by suicide, your death will occur when your current purpose in this current earth cycle is finished.

Will you come back in another earth body at some-time? Probably, but not necessarily. Whether you need to come back, or choose to come back, depends on where you are in your own personal evolvement as an intelligent, spiritual energy.

What happens after your container dies? Many books are available on this subject, so I won't belabor it here. Suffice it to say that life is a continuous chain of learning and experiencing, whether in a body in this earth plane or in some other plane with or without a body.

But what about the dying experience itself that we will all have when we exit our current earth life cycle?

Is it painful? No, it is not. Yes, there may well be pain leading up to the death of the container due to injury or illness, but I know of no reason to believe the death experience itself has any discomfort at all. On the contrary, death seems to be a pleasant release of the "pain" of this earth life. None of the clients I regressed ever had any pain associated with death. Nor have I experienced any discomfort during regression through a previous death. I have read that some who have studied death more than I have believe that the self (the real you) exits the body before the actual death of the body. And it is an easy, painless exit.

Some years ago I pondered this whole question of death in several meditation sessions. I was looking for some answer to put everything into perspective for me. I didn't receive an immediate awareness during the meditation, but several weeks later I had an unusual experience that gave me the perspective I was looking for. I will share that experience with you now, and maybe it will put dying into perspective for you, too.

One day the postman delivered a letter addressed to me. It had no return address, and the postmark was so obliterated that it was impossible for me to determine where the letter had been mailed from. Inside the envelope was a single sheet of paper with some words typed on it. There was nothing on the paper to indicate the source of the words.

These were those words:

"I am standing upon the seashore, and a ship at my side spreads her white sails to the morning breeze and sets out for the blue ocean. She is an object of beauty and strength, and I stand and watch her until at length she hangs like a tiny speck out there where the sky and sea seem to mingle with each other. At that moment, someone at my side said, `There, she's gone!'

"Gone? Gone where? Gone from my sight, that is all. For she is just as large in mast and hull and spar as she was when she left my side, and just as able to carry her load of living freight to the point of destination. Her diminished size is in me, not in her. And at that moment when someone at my side had said, `There, she's gone!' there were other eyes watching her come and other voices ready to take up the glad shout, `There, she comes!' And that is dying."

Because death is an absolute, necessary, and inevitable experience for all of us, we should build a bridge to it so that when we cross over to the other side we will be where we want to be in our evolutionary process.

How do we do it?

You have probably heard the adage, "Live each day as though you were going to die tomorrow." That is exactly how you build your bridge to your death experience.

Do not attempt to determine how, when, and where you will die. Those things will take care of themselves as a natural result of how you live each day.

Live each day, one at a time, with integrity, love, hope, enthusiasm, and always doing the very best you can do within the realm of your ability and circumstance. In doing this, you will have built a good bridge to tomorrow when it is time to depart this earthly existence. And the bridge will be exactly the right bridge to take you to exactly where you should be.

# Chapter 24

# Far Out

*The best cosmetic in the world is an active
mind that is always finding something new.*
                              Mary Meek Atkeson

We all know people whose body is alive but who have
been mentally dead for years. They walk around and go
through the motions of living, but they can't remember
the last time they had an original thought or a creative
idea. Typically their idea of excitement is to watch television, sleep, eat, and repeat this cycle every day. Their
favorite topic of conversation is the weather.

Their mind is as active as a dead battery.

The tragedy is that no one has to be that way. The
reality is that any one of us can become that way if we
don't keep our minds active.

You absolutely must have an active mind in order to
build bridges to tomorrow. It is a prerequisite.

Shortly I will show you three unusual (paranormal) ways to activate your mind and to stretch your
mind to new dimensions. But first let's look at some

simple, normal everyday things you can do to keep your mind active.

The most important is to develop and pursue more than one outlet for your energies—have a hobby. The person who devotes all his/her time to one activity, usually a job, is in danger of stagnating their mind. Agreed, some jobs are so exciting and have so many facets that your mind is always kept active, challenged, and satisfied. Name one. I am not able to at the moment, but surely there must be some.

I am a writer, and writing is a tremendous mental challenge. I love writing, but I would go bonkers if that was all I did. So I also practice astrology, travel extensively for pleasure, practice hypnosis, give lectures, collect elephants (miniatures, not live ones), read voraciously, meditate, and do a couple other things. I keep my mind active, and I am an active, successful bridge-builder.

One of the things I do to keep my mind active is to memorize pieces of information that I like or that I think might be of value to me. Here are just a few of the things I've memorized to stretch my mind and keep it active: The Declaration of Independence, "Gunga Din" (an 84-line poem), various passages from the Rubaiyat of Omar Khayyam, many of the passages in this book, hours of hypnosis routines, the presidents of the United States in order, "The Face On The Barroom Floor" (poem), "The Winds of Fate" (poem), and literally hundreds of other poems, quotations, and facts. I have given two-hour lectures and five-hour workshops entirely from memory, without repeating anything.

The more you memorize, the easier it becomes and the faster you can do it. It is a great mind stretcher that anyone can do with a little effort. I recommend you start doing it.

Start with the sixteen-word quotation at the beginning of this chapter. A simple task. Then pick some other quotations at the beginning of other chapters and memorize them. This is an excellent beginning to stretch your mind and keep it active. Once you make this a habit, it becomes fun, and it is tremendously beneficial.

Additionally, I recommend you develop a hobby if you don't already have one. There are thousands to choose from. Needlework, stamp collecting, collecting coins or anything else for that matter, antiques, coaching little league, crafts of all sorts, teaching adult education classes. The list is endless. Just pick something that interests you and do it. Spend as little or as much time as you choose. The only requisite is that it is an activity that allows a different channel from your usual channel for your mind to stretch and be active.

The great football player, Roosevelt Greer, has a hobby doing needlepoint. That certainly is a different channel than his usual activity, and it keeps his mind honed.

No—television watching does not qualify as a bonafide hobby. Television, per se, does not stretch the mind. Television has a tendency to anesthetize the mind rather than expand it. And, no, I am not knocking television. Television is a great source of entertainment, information, and enjoyment. Just put television into proper perspective in your life.

Now let's explore some unusual mind stretchers.

The balance of this chapter is slightly off-center from the rest of this book. The rest of this book is sound, practical, and rational—pretty much "normal."

But if you want to really progress, you must start stretching your mind to encompass possibilities beyond what you consider normal. You must be willing to test the implausible.

It is the very act of testing, exploring, and evaluating possibilities that you consider to be impossible or implausible that allows your mind and your knowledge to expand. When you examine the impossible, you sometimes discover that it *is possible*. Sometimes you merely reaffirm that indeed it *is impossible*.

The conclusion you reach isn't nearly as important as the fact that you had the guts and open-mindedness to examine what was seemingly implausible in the first place. One of the primary purposes of this book is to motivate you to think—to not be timid about trying something, and making up your own mind based on your own experience.

In this chapter, I offer three methods of finding out information that most people "normally" do not use or even have enough spirit of adventure to try. For some people, these methods (tools) work extremely well and furnish a great deal of valuable, accurate information. For other people, these tools do not work especially well at all. What your results may be, I have no idea. I do know that the more open-minded and light-hearted you are, the better your chances for success.

The more information you have, the better able you are to construct your bridges to tomorrow. It is in this spirit that I present the following tools to you—that you may use them to obtain more information and build better bridges.

In all three cases, I have no idea how or why they work. I just know from my own experience that they do work. I am not one to get hung up on technical or scientific proof for things. If they work for me, I use them. If they don't work for me, I abandon them. Gravity works—I don't know how or why and I don't really care—I just use it to my advantage.

Electricity works—I don't know how or why and I don't really care—I just use it to my advantage. So it is with the following three tools.

## The Dictionary Game

Use this tool when you want to find one word that will provide an accurate answer to a question you have in mind. To use this tool, set a closed dictionary in front of you on a table. Out loud, ask your question. Then close your eyes and open the dictionary randomly and put your finger at any place on one of the two open pages.

Then open your eyes and read the word your finger is pointing to and the definitions for that word. This information will either answer your question directly or will provide information that will lead to the answer.

Here are two examples of how I used the dictionary game to get accurate information.

**Example #1:** A friend used swing rods and a pendulum all the time, and he said they were accurate. He recommended that I try them. Quite frankly, I was skeptical.

When I was alone, I placed my closed dictionary on my desk and asked out loud, "Can swing rods or a pendulum be beneficial tools for me to use to obtain correct answers to all my questions?"

Then I closed my eyes. I opened and closed the dictionary several times. I riffled through pages. Finally I had a feeling, so I stopped flipping pages and I put the index finger of my right hand someplace on the left page.

I opened my eyes. My finger was on the word "potentiality." The definition: 1) Inherent capacity for growth, development, or coming into existence. 2) Something possessing potentiality.

This clearly told me to start using swing rods and a pendulum because they could be potentially beneficial tools for me.

**Example #2:** A company I was writing technical material for was embroiled in a costly political situation. The company had a valid contract with the Department of Energy to ship nuclear waste to a repository in another state. The governor of that state refused to allow the shipment to enter the state.

After a year of political wrangling, a meeting was scheduled on January 11, 1991 to resolve the problem. The day before, on January 10, I played my dictionary game.

I asked, "What will be the result of tomorrow's meeting regarding our nuclear shipment?"

I closed my eyes, opened the dictionary, and put my finger on one of the pages.

The word I had selected was "overturn," which I felt told me that the governor's stance would be overturned. That is exactly what happened, and the Department of Energy told our company we could ship the nuclear waste. Unfortunately several weeks later a legal matter arose which prevented the shipment. But the dictionary had given me the correct answer to my question.

I think you can see how this dictionary game could be beneficial to you in your quest for information.

### Swing Rods

A dowser is a person who locates underground water or minerals by using a divining rod. The divining rod is usually either a V-shaped piece of twig from a tree or a swing rod.

Figure A.  Swing Rods

My swing rods are shown in figure A. I had some scrap heavy-gauge wire (steel alloy, I think) that I had hoarded in the garage for years. I cut two pieces, each 26 inches long, and bent them so the handle was 7-1/2 inches long and the the pointer was 18-1/2 inches long. The length and handle-to-pointer ratio are not important; that is just how I happened to make it. I suspect copper wire would be even better, but I didn't have any and it was too expensive to buy to make a tool that I didn't think would work anyway. You can also make a very good swing rod from a wire clothes-hanger.

I use two plastic drinking straws as sleeves for the handles. That allows the rods to swing freely because my hands do not touch the rods, which prevents me from deliberately controlling the rods with my hands. In figure A, one swing rod has the plastic straw over the handle. The other rod has its plastic straw laying next to the handle for illustration.

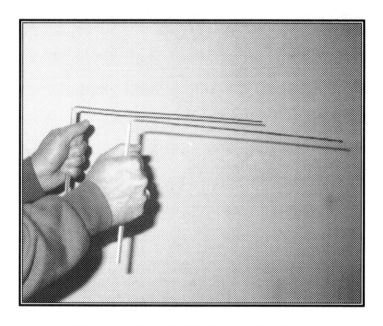

Figure B.   How To Hold The Swing Rods

I hold the rods as shown in figure B. Then I ask my question. If the answer is yes, the rods both swing inward toward me. If the answer is no, both rods swing outward away from me.

You need to develop skill in asking the right questions in order to get accurate answers. For example, if you ask, "Will I get a salary increase?," a yes answer really doesn't tell you much. "When?" and "How much?" are what you really want to know.

I am still a neophyte with the swing rods and most of my problems stem from not asking the right questions. When I do use a good questioning technique, I get accurate information.

Here is a recent situation where I didn't know all the right questions to ask so I didn't find out what I wanted to know.

A black woman reported her home vandalized. Swastikas were painted all over her walls, and the rooms were a mess. Of course, the investigation immediately focused on hate groups.

When I read about it in the newspaper I decided to use my swing rods to find out who did it.

I mentioned various hate groups by name and asked if they were responsible. I got all "NO" answers. I then asked if it was a neighbor, again a "NO" answer. Was it someone who didn't like her personally; a "NO" answer. Was it just malicious mischief by some kids; "NO again. Was someone attempting to burglarize her home; "NO" again.

Now I was confused. The swing rods said no one did it to her, so I figured the swing rods were giving me wrong answers, and I put them away.

Five days later the woman was arrested. She had done it to herself, in an insurance fraud scheme to collect money for the damage.

The swing rods had been right all along, but I didn't know how to ask the right questions to solve the problem. I had quit too soon. It had never occurred to me to ask if she had done it to herself .

Learn from my mistake.

I have also had fun with my swing rods. For example, I held them straight out as shown in figure B and then said, "I want the left rod to point to my bookcase and the right rod to point to my computer." The rods swung unerringly to do exactly what I had commanded.

Without a doubt there is much more power and value for me to explore in using my swing rods. I have barely begun.

Why not try it?

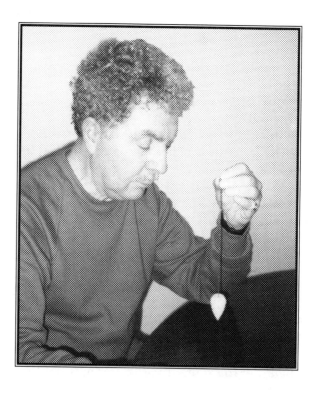

Figure C.  The Pendulum

## *The Pendulum*

Figure C shows me holding my pendulum in the proper position for asking questions. Like the swing rods, the pendulum can answer only questions that can be answered by either a "yes" or "no."

Figure D shows the direction the pendulum moves for me to give answers: swinging alternately to me and then away from me, sort of like a nodding head, for a "yes" answer; swinging side to side, sort of like a shaking head, for a "no" answer. If it swings in a circular motion clockwise, it means I need to rephrase the question.

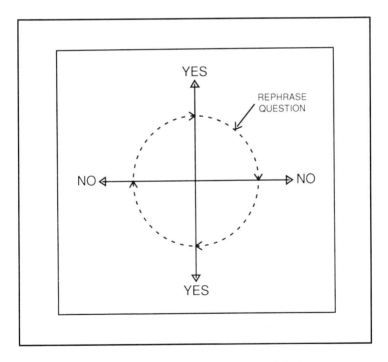

Figure D.  Pendulum's Answering Motion

Just like the swing rods, you need to build some experience with asking questions in order to get the best results.

You don't need a professional type pendulum as I have in figure C. Just use a string or thread with a small weight on one end to serve as the pendulum. A button, a nut or bolt, a small stone, a piece of metal or wood, etc. will do just fine for your pendulum.

I am still a neophyte at using the pendulum, but so far I've gotten impressive results.

I am still in the exploratory stage with the three tools discussed in this chapter. So far I've gotten better results from the dictionary than from the swing rods and the pendulum.

The swing rods and the pendulum have given me mixed results, but there seems to be good potential because I get more correct answers than incorrect ones. Also part of the problem is my lack of good questioning technique.

When I suggest you experiment with these tools, I do so in the spirit of exercising your mind so it will be more inclined to embrace new thoughts. If in the process you discover tools that are useful to you—great—use them. If not, discard them.

It is the process of exercising your mind that is important, to enable it to build better bridges. Physical exercise strengthens your body, and mental and spiritual exercise strengthen your mind.

I have tested the implausible many times in the past, and continue to do so nearly every day. I expect to constantly stretch my mind throughout the rest of my life, by exploring new horizons that only appear to be unattainable.

Here are just a few of the more bizarre avenues I have explored in my quest for mind expansion:

- Investigated and performed psychic healing and found that it does work.

- Performed communication with deceased persons and mental communication with living persons and had success in both areas.

- Performed standard ESP (extra-sensory perception) tests using decks of cards with symbols on them and cards with colors on them. I consistently scored well above, "guess factor" on these.

- Projected my intelligence psychically to cause things to happen.

In the process of these investigations I became somewhat of an authority on paranormal experience, and I wrote a book about it. If you really want to pull out all the stops in your quest to stretch your mind, you might want to get my book and read it.

A person's mind, once stretched to accommodate a new idea, never returns to its original dimensions.

Why not give it a try?

Chapter 25

# Become a
# Committee of One

*Life truly lived is a risky business, and if one
puts up too many fences against risk one ends
by shutting out life itself.*
                                    Kenneth S. Davis

God created man, and man created committees. Committees are one of man's worst inventions.

When God creates a horse, it looks like a horse. When a committee creates a horse, it looks like a camel.

When man created committees he had the best of intentions. The concept of a committee is good. The idea is to solve a problem or create something new by naming a number of capable people to serve on a committee to do it. It certainly is much simpler than trying to have the entire population solve the problem.

And once in a blue moon a committee actually does succeed in solving a problem properly or in creating something new that makes sense. To put this into perspective, a blue moon occurs approximately once every 2-1/2 years, when there are two full moons in the same calendar month. Not a very good average for success, is it?

On any given day, you need only to read the newspaper or watch the television news to observe the results of government committees in action. It would be laughable if it weren't so serious, in terms of money wasted, grief imposed on people, and screw-ups in general. You may recall the congressional committee hearings on the confirmation of U.S. Supreme Court Justice Clarence Thomas. What a tragic farce that was.

Government runs by committee. So do most organizations. If you work for a fairly large company, or if you are affiliated with some organization (i.e., PTA, Lion's Club, etc.) the chances are that you have, or will, serve on a committee at some time.

It may be a committee to organize a company picnic or devise a better school lunch menu. It makes no difference. The odds are that the outcome will be more costly, less desirable, and the brunt of more complaints than if just one person made all the decisions.

Why is it that committee results are often so unsuccessful? They are unsuccessful because more than one person is on the committee. That means more than one viewpoint is entered into the problem. The more people, the more opinions, and hence the greater the problem. In order to reach a conclusion, each committee member must compromise some portion of his/her viewpoint so that one common viewpoint can be reached. That means that most likely none of the committee members is 100% satisfied with the results.

A strange phenomenon occurs when a committee is formed.

Perfectly normal, intelligent, competent people are selected to serve on the committee, and they are given a mission to accomplish. Memos are issued informing everyone of the committee, their purpose, and their names.

The committee members begin to act important and talk differently—they substitute rhetoric for plain talk. Their get-togethers become mass meetings of muddled minds. They get defensive about their ideas, which continually become vaguer, and they are overly sensitive to the remarks of the other committee members. Arguments and hostilities erupt.

By their third meeting (sometimes sooner), their brains go out to lunch for the duration of the committee's existence, and they begin to display the habits of the mythical Munga-Munga bird.

The mythical Munga-Munga bird, for those of you who may not know, is a bird that flies in ever decreasing concentric circles until it flies up its own backside. That gives you some idea where committee members' heads are located.

So it is no wonder that the results of most committees range from stupid to disastrous.

Committees are a perfect forum for spreading responsibility and blame. If things go right, each committee member takes the credit—everything was their idea. If, however, things do not turn out so good, each member absolves him/herself of any blame or responsibility with a statement like, "It wasn't my idea. I was against it from the start, but I was out-voted."

There is an axiom about committees: The magnitude of screw-ups is directly proportional to the number of people on the committee. In addition, committees are self-perpetuating; once you create a committee, it is nearly impossible to get rid of it.

Here is a hypothetical example of a typical committee in action. The company president appoints a five-member committee to select the color of the walls for the corporate conference room.

Member #1 loves red, but hates any shade of blue. Member #2 loves orange, but hates red and green. Member #3 likes dark earthtones, but hates any bright colors, especially yellows or purple hues. Member #4 likes lavender and hates earthtones. Member #5 doesn't like anything the other members like. After much discussion the only color no one hates is black. They are not especially fond of black, but they don't hate it. So black is their compromise selection.

Can you imagine the president's reaction when he or she walks into a black conference room?

This example is a bit ridiculous to be sure, but it illustrates the danger of committee decisions.

The tragedy is that many people live their lives as a result of committee decisions. Example: The boy graduating from high school wants to accept the offer from the Detroit Tigers to join their farm team. He is an outstanding athlete and wants to try being a professional. But the committee has other ideas. The committee is his mother, father, and girl friend.

The girl friend says, "You would be traveling a lot. That is no way for a marriage to work. I want to settle down and have a family. If you go with the Tigers, I will not marry you or wait for you."

The father says, "It probably won't work out and you will have wasted all those years on a farm team when you could have gotten a college degree and made a sensible lifelong career as a doctor or lawyer."

The mother says, "This is just a foolish dream. Playing games is for children. You are an adult now and you must start thinking like one. You must get married and assume a responsible position in society."

The chances are good that this young man will cave in to the wishes of the committee and ruin his life, or at least follow a path in life that is tolerable but not the exciting one he could have had.

How sad!

Every time you allow a committee to make your decisions for you, you build a bridge to somewhere that you would rather not be. A lot of people allow this, and they are unhappy and unfulfilled.

You have a right to be happy and fulfilled. You have a right to pursue your dreams. You have a right to build your own bridges, by yourself, to wherever you want. And you have a right to make your own mistakes without someone else's assistance.

In order for you to exercise those rights, you must listen only to a committee of one, and that one committee member must be you.

You alone must build your own bridges, you must accept responsibility for them, and you will reap the results of them. That is the only way bridge-building can span the distance to the tomorrow that you want.

Almost always there are plenty of committee members hanging around, ready to help you run your life. If you let them, and things turn out wrong, they don't care. Why should they care? It is your life that is messed up—not theirs.

If you let the committee help and things turn out well, they will be first in line to take credit for it. They will relegate you to a position of being a puppet, and they will be the puppeteer. They pull the strings, and you jump.

There is one advantage of allowing a committee to pull your strings—you relieve yourself of the risk of making your own decisions—you remove some of the risk in your life.

The disadvantage of not pulling your own strings is that you really don't live at all. You merely exist. You eat, sleep, go to work—all by rote—no excitement—no zest for living.

Life is to be lived, folks! That means taking risks! So what? Wake up and smell the roses! Start pulling your own strings!

Dead fish can only swim with the current. Live fish can swim in any direction they choose. Think about it.

Make yourself a committee of one exclusively, to run your own life, to build your own bridges, and to really live life to the fullest.

Of course, you will make mistakes, but that is okay. They are your mistakes and you can live with that and learn from it. It is really tough to live with someone else's mistakes.

Never fear risk. To fear risk is to fence out the potential quality of life you deserve. Respect risk, use your bridges to take calculated risks, not foolhardy risks, and you will do just fine.

This does not mean that you should ignore good advice. By all means, there are times when it makes sense to consult with other people. If you want to invest your money, consult with investment professionals. If you have a legal problem, consult a lawyer. And so forth. But, for pete's sake, make your own decisions yourself. Don't take a consensus. Don't take a poll. Don't cave in to what others think is best for you. In most cases, when others say, "You should do this for your own good," they really mean you should do it for *their* good.

To build your bridges to tomorrow: Ride your own horse, pull your own strings, and follow the decisions of the committee of one, of which you are the only committee member.

# Chapter 26

# Good Ol' Boys

*Courage is the first of human qualities because
it is the quality which guarantees all the others.*
Winston Churchill

Good Ol' Boy networks are alive and well in every part
of this country and in every facet of society, and they
can be a serious detriment to you if you try to build a
bridge into some domain that they consider sacred to
themselves.

"Good Ol' Boy" is a certain type of mentality that is
stagnated and frozen in time and that refuses to recognize truth, justice, or new thoughts. Only their way of
thinking and acting is acceptable.

When a Good Ol' Boy network exists in positions of
power, it can wreak major havoc on anyone who dares to
defy the network.

An illustration can be found nearly every day in
the newspaper or on the television news. Example: A
worker in the Department of Defense blows the whistle
on kickbacks and bribes accepted by certain officials
from contractors.

The worker is telling the truth, but what really happens? The Good Ol' Boy network in the Department of Defense and in the contractors' hallowed halls swings into action. The Good Ol' Boys stick together and fabricate lies and exercise their power against the worker who is acting as a good citizen. The worker is skinned and hung out to dry. The worker is blasphemed and discredited. The worker is fired and blackballed from getting another decent job.

The Good Ol' Boys go scott free—unscathed—free to continue their misdeeds.

Good Ol' Boys waste taxpayers' money by diverting it to their personal interests.

Good Ol' Boys, in general, do whatever they can to impede progress. They live and think in a frozen, outdated period of time, and they resist any change that does not personally benefit them.

I don't think I need to beat on this further. The point is made that the Good Ol' Boys are a detriment.

As you plan and build your bridges, you may occasionally encounter a Good Ol' Boy network. Good Ol' Boys can be defeated if you are not naive, and if you build your bridge properly, and if you refuse to cave in to their pressures.

In Chapter 19 of this book, I recounted a true story of how I defeated a small town Good Ol' Boy network that had refused to let my wife register to vote.

Bridge-building is not for the faint hearted. It takes guts and a deep desire to achieve the life you want and deserve. If you have a tendency to cave in to intimidation I recommend you first build a bridge to overcome it. Build a bridge to make yourself strong, confident, resolute, and courageous.

I like the way Robert Louis Stevenson said it:

*The world has no room for cowards. We must all be ready somehow to toil, to suffer, to die. And yours is not the less because no drum beats before you when you go out to your daily battlefields, and no crowds shout your coming when you return from your daily victory and defeat.*

Nothing can stop one good person who has a good cause and just keeps on coming. Burn that into your mind until it becomes a living part of you. Then Good Ol' Boys won't stand a chance.

# Chapter 27

# What Kind of Bridge-Builder are You?

*A person's ultimate freedom is the ability to choose one's attitude in any given set of circumstances.*

Victor Frankl

Your bridge-building will be a success in the exact measure that you think you deserve it to be.

In other words, your bridge-building relates directly to your self-esteem (self-image)—your own opinion of yourself—what you think and feel about yourself—what you think you can do. Other people's opinions about you do not count at all unless you deliberately choose to let them count.

I personally do not allow others to have a vote in matters that pertain to my self-esteem and my bridge-building. When I first started out to be a successful writer, not one person stood by my side with an encouraging word. However, I did receive many discouraging words. If I had allowed those people's vote to count, I would never have succeeded. But I chose to let only my vote count—I knew I could succeed, and I did.

For your success as a bridge-builder and as a happy human being, I suggest you start right now to build a powerful, positive self-esteem. Once you do that, your own powerful vote will cancel out all adversity.

To help you tailor your self-esteem, the remainder of this chapter contains a listing of key positive and negative tendencies in self-esteems. First identify the qualities that pertain to you now. Then concentrate on eliminating the negative ones by building bridges to the positive ones so they become the real you.

Often the act of eliminating a negative tendency automatically brings the positive tendency to reality. For example, you are extremely shy and don't want to be. You take a course in public speaking, which causes you to overcome the shyness and at the same time gives you self-confidence, a positive trait.

Dale Carnegie taught, "Act enthusiastic and you will be enthusiastic." The premise in this teaching is that if you force yourself to act in a manner that you wish you possessed, you will achieve the very thing you are acting out. Act brave, and you become brave. Act confident, and you become confident. Act happy, and you become happy. And so forth.

Keep these things in mind as you read the list of traits and begin constructing your personal bridges to change. Become an actor playing a part, and eventually you will become the part, and it won't be acting anymore—it will be the new real you.

Remember that success is not measured from where you stand, but from how far you have come from where you started.

## *Key Self-Image Traits*

| Positive Tendencies | Negative Tendencies |
|---|---|
| + self-affirming | − self-critical |
| + self-respecting | − puts unreal demands on self |
| + self-forgiving | − perfectionist |
| + confident | − self-conscious |
| + enthusiastic | − self-pitying |
| + energetic | − self-condemning |
| + ambitious | − feels inferior |
| + self-motivating | − feels like a failure |
| + productive | − expects to fail |
| + successful | − fearful |
| + optimistic | − vulnerable to what others think |
| + feels equal to others | − people-pleaser |
| + accepts self and others | − dependent |
| + has satisfying relationships with others | − seeks outside recognition |
| + caring for others | − feels guilty |
| + ability to love and be loved | − defensive |
| + thinks independently | − angry |
| + makes and acts on decisions | − indecisive |
| + courage to stand up for own convictions | − tends to be unsure |
| + assertive | − over-responsive to praise |
| + risking | − shy |
| + venturesome | − timid |
| + flexible | − tends to listen rather than participate |
| + spontaneous | − pessimistic about competitive situations |
| + eager to get involved | − loner, isolated, lonely |

## *Key Self-Image Traits*

| Positive Tendencies | Negative Tendencies |
| --- | --- |
| + gregarious | – hypersensitive to criticism |
| + handles criticism | – rigid |
| + accepts praise without embarrassment | – fanatic |
| + experiences range of feelings | – cantankerous, quarrelsome |
| + open | – sarcastic |
| + well aware of strengths, shortcomings, weaknesses | – pessimistic |
| + capable of self-improvement | – cynical, distrusting, skeptic |
| + actualizing | – disinterested in body and appearance |
| + autonomous | – self-denial |
| + able to cope with day-to-day demands | – often unhealthy |
| + high tolerance level of frustration | – procrastinates |
| + perseveres in face of adversity | – non-productive |
| + efficient perception of reality | – bored |
| + physically healthy | – tense |
| + relaxed | – confused |
| + sexually drawn to people | – feels unloved |
| + liked and admired | – excessive daydreaming |
| + makes good appearance | – hypercritical of others |
| + maintains pleasant surroundings | – lacks ability to give honest praise |
| + thoughtful | –– blames others |
| + poised | – rationalizes |

## Key Self-Image Traits

| Positive Tendencies | Negative Tendencies |
| --- | --- |
| + sense of humor | – absorbed in self |
| + attracted to others with high self-esteem | – selfish |
| + integrated | – fatigued |
| | – inappropriate voice quality |
| | – poor posture and body movement |
| | – subject to depression |
| | – may be suicidal |
| | – lives through heroes |
| | – name dropper |
| | – jealous |
| | – possessive |
| | – risk avoider |
| | – puts up false front |
| | – greedy |
| | – over indulges |
| | – arrogant, superior attitude |
| | – overly aggressive |
| | – overbearing |
| | – rebels against authority |
| | – compulsive achiever |
| | – preoccupied with body and appearances |

# Chapter 28

# Don't Cross Bridges Before You Build Them

*The secret of success is consistency of purpose.*
Benjamin Disraeli

Bridge-building is a systematic sequence of thoughts, events, and actions that leads to a desired result or destination.

The title of this chapter wisely advises you to not attempt to reach the destination (i.e., cross the bridge) if you have not first completed all of the steps to complete the bridge. If you try to cross an uncompleted bridge, you will fail to reach your destination and will create problems for yourself and possibly for others also.

For example: You are building a bridge to become a registered nurse. This requires money, self-discipline, determination, completing a prescribed course of study from an accredited nursing school, a graduation diploma, and a legal license from your state of residence.

A year before your graduation, you decide to skip the rest and just set yourself up as a nurse because you need the income. You take private nursing patients only, and pass yourself off as a licensed nurse. It is easy to do that—it happens every day.

The moment you do that, you put your patients at risk, because there was an additional year of schooling that you didn't take. Thus, there are many things you don't know that you need to know. You could cause someone to die because of your ignorance.

You also put yourself at great risk for civil and criminal charges. At the very least, you set the stage for great personal financial loss; and at worst, for a jail sentence. And you certainly set yourself up for being shamed in front of the whole community.

It isn't worth it, is it?

You can devise other scenarios for your own situation if you cross bridges before they are completed. The result will be failure of some sort.

# Chapter 29

# **Bridge Completed**

*Ah, great it is to believe the dream*
*As we stand in youth by the starry stream;*
*But a greater thing is to fight life through,*
*And say at the end, "The dream is true!"*
Edward Markham

This book has twenty-nine chapters, each one of which is a small bridge I have built. Combined, they make up the large bridge—this book—which I committed to myself to write. I wanted to write something that would make you stop and think seriously about yourself and your life. I wanted to make you understand that you have every right to think for yourself, and to be successful and happy. I wanted to suggest some how-to methods as tools for you as readers to use to build your own bridges. I wanted to let you know that you do not have to tolerate intolerance; to let you know that you do have choices, and that you are the captain of your own ship.

This book is part philosophy, part psychology, and part how-to techniques for improving your life. It blends the esoteric with the practical to show you a wide spectrum of opportunities available to you, to help you shape your future the way you want it to be. There is something for everyone here, if you care to recognize it and use it.

This book challenges you to think for yourself, to consider new ideas, some of which may be "off the wall" to your current way of thinking. This book presents options and possibilities but does not force anything down your throat you. You alone make the choices that affect you.

*Bridges to Success and Fulfillment* is my bridge to achieve those things in the preceding paragraphs. I hope it helps you to build bridges to success and fulfillment for yourself.

I close with the words of Robert Frost, "I am not a teacher, but an awakener."

## STAY IN TOUCH

On the following pages you will find some of the books now available on related subjects. Your book dealer stocks most of these and will stock new titles in the Llewellyn series as they become available. We urge your patronage.

To obtain our full catalog, to keep informed about new titles as they are released and to benefit from informative articles and helpful news, you are invited to write for our bimonthly news magazine/catalog, *Llewellyn's New Worlds of Mind and Spirit*. A sample copy is free, and it will continue coming to you at no cost as long as you are an active mail customer. Or you may subscribe for just $7.00 in the U.S.A. and Canada ($20.00 overseas, first class mail). Many bookstores also have *New Worlds* available to their customers. Ask for it.

**Llewellyn's New Worlds of Mind and Spirit**
**P.O. Box 64383-323, St. Paul, MN 55164-0383, U.S.A.**
* * *

### TO ORDER BOOKS AND TAPES

If your book dealer does not have the books described, you may order them directly from the publisher by sending full price in U.S. funds, plus $3.00 for postage and handling for orders *under* $10.00; $4.00 for orders *over* $10.00. There are no postage and handling charges for orders over $50.00. Postage and handling rates are subject to change. We ship UPS whenever possible. Delivery guaranteed. Provide your street address as UPS does not deliver to P.O. Boxes. UPS to Canada requires a $50.00 minimum order. Allow 4-6 weeks for delivery. Orders outside the U.S.A. and Canada: Airmail—add retail price of book; add $5.00 for each non-book item (tapes, etc.); add $1.00 per item for surface mail.

### FOR GROUP STUDY AND PURCHASE

Because there is a great deal of interest in group discussion and study of the subject matter of this book, we offer a special quantity price to group leaders or agents. Our Special Quantity Price for a minimum order of five copies of *Bridges to Success & Fulfillment* is $23.85 cash-with-order. This price includes postage and handling within the United States. Minnesota residents must add 6.5% sales tax. For additional quantities, please order in multiples of five. For Canadian and foreign orders, add postage and handling charges as above. Credit card (VISA, MasterCard, American Express) orders are accepted. Charge card orders only ($15.00 minimum order) may be phoned in free within the U.S.A. or Canada by dialing 1-800-THE-MOON. For customer service, call 1-612-291-1970. Mail orders to:

**LLEWELLYN PUBLICATIONS**
**P.O. Box 64383-323, St. Paul, MN 55164-0383, U.S.A.**

**BEYOND HYPNOSIS**
**A Program for Developing Your Psychic & Healing Powers**
**by William Hewitt**
This book contains a complete system for using hypnosis to enter a beneficial altered state of consciousness in order to develop your psychic abilities. Here is a 30-day program (just 10 to 20 minutes per day is all it takes!) to release your psychic awareness and then hone it to a fine skill through a series of mental exercises that anyone can do!

*Beyond Hypnosis* lets you make positive changes in your life. You will find yourself doing things that you only dreamed about in the past, including easy and safe out-of-body travel and communication with spiritual, nonphysical entities. Speed up your learning and reading abilities and retain more of the information you study. A must for students of all kinds! *Beyond Hypnosis* shows you how to create your own reality, how to reshape your own life and the lives of others—and ultimately how to reshape the world and beyond what we call this world! This book will introduce you to a beneficial altered state of consciousness which is achieved by using your own natural abilities to control your mind. It is in this state where you will learn to expand your psychic abilities beyond belief!
**0-87542-305-1, 240 pgs., 5 1/4 x 8, softcover**                 **$7.95**

**HYPNOSIS**
**A Power Program for Self-Improvement, Changing Your Life and Helping Others**
**by William W. Hewitt**
There is no other hypnosis book on the market that has the depth, scope, and explicit detail as does this book. The exact and complete wording of dozens of hypnosis routines is given. Real case histories and examples are included for a broad spectrum of situations. Precise instructions for achieving self-hypnosis, the alpha state, and theta state are given. There are dozens of hypnotic suggestions given covering virtually any type of situation one might encounter. The book tells how to become a professional hypnotist. It tells how to become expert at self-hypnosis all by yourself without external help. And it even contains a short dissertation going "beyond hypnosis" into the realm of psychic phenomena. There is something of value here for nearly everyone.

This book details exactly how to gain all you want to enrich your life at every level. No matter how simple or how profound your goals, this book teaches you how to realize them. The book is not magic; it is a powerful key to unlock the magic within each of us.
**0-87542-300-0, 192 pgs., 5 1/4 x 8, softcover**                 **$7.95**

Prices subject to change without notice.

## SELF-HYPNOSIS AUDIOTAPES
**by professional hypnotherapist William Hewitt**
Change your subconscious in a safe and easy way that gets results. Use these tapes in the comfort of your own home to change your life for the better—permanently!

### Your Perfect Weight Through Self-Hypnosis
Change the behaviors responsible for unwanted weight gain. Whether you need to shed extra pounds or just learn to control your appetite and eating habits, William Hewitt offers hypnosis techniques to help you get the body you want!
**0-87542-338-8, 45 min.**                               **$9.95**

### Become Smoke Free Through Self-Hypnosis
Non-smoker. Easy to say, but it can seem impossible to do. This tape helps you get to the roots of why you smoke, and helps you break the nicotine habit.
**0-87542-339-6, 45 min.**                               **$9.95**

### Relaxation and Stress Management Through Self-Hypnosis
Stress has been named as a leading cause of many health problems including depression and heart disease. While you can't eliminate stress completely, through self-hypnosis you can learn to control it before it takes its toll on you.
**0-87542-335-3, 45 min.**                               **$9.95**

### The Psychic Workout Through Self-Hypnosis
Rid your mind of negativity and anger, and fill it with love, faith, forgiveness and positivity with this winning combination of self-hypnosis and creative visualization.
**0-87542-340-X, 60 min.**                               **$9.95**

## ASTROLOGY FOR BEGINNERS
### An Easy Guide to Understanding & Interpreting Your Chart
### by William Hewitt

Anyone who is interested in astrology will enjoy *Astrology for Beginners*. This book makes astrology easy and exciting by presenting all of the basics in an orderly sequence while focusing on the natal chart. Llewellyn even includes a coupon for a free computerized natal chart so you can begin interpretations almost immediately without complicated mathematics.

*Astrology for Beginners* covers all of the basics. Learn exactly what astrology is and how it works. Explore signs, planets, houses and aspects. Learn how to interpret a birth chart. Discover the meaning of transits, predictive astrology and progressions. Determine your horoscope chart in minutes without using math.

Whether you want to practice astrology for a hobby or aspire to become a professional astrologer, *Astrology for Beginners* is the book you need to get started on the right track.

**0-87542-307-8, 288 pgs., 5 1/4 x 8, softcover**       **$7.95**

## TEA LEAF READING
### by William W. Hewitt

There may be more powerful methods of divination than tea leaf reading, but they also require heavy-duty commitment and disciplined training. Fun, lighthearted, and requiring very little discipline, tea leaf reading asks only of its practitioners an open mind and a spirit of adventure.

Just one cup of tea can give you a 12-month prophecy, or an answer to a specific question. It can also be used to examine the past. There is no regimen needed, no complicated rules to memorize. Simply read the instructions and look up the meanings of the symbols!

*Tea Leaf Reading* explains the how it works, how to prepare the cup for reading, how to analyze and read tea leaf symbols, how to interpret the symbols you see. It provides an extensive glossary of symbols with their meanings so you can begin interpretations immediately; it provides an index, with cross-references for quick location of the symbols in the glossary; and it has an appendix of crystals and metals that can aid you in reading tea leaves and in other pursuits.

**0-87542-308-6, 240 pgs., mass market**       **$3.95**

Prices subject to change without notice.

## THE SECRET WAY OF WONDER
**Insights from the Silence**
**by Guy Finley**
**Introduction by Desi Arnaz, Jr.**
Discover an inner world of wisdom and make miracles happen! Here is a simple yet deeply effective system of illuminating and eliminating the problems of inner mental and emotional life.

*The Secret Way of Wonder* is an interactive spiritual workbook, offering guided practice for self-study. It is about Awakening the Power of Wonder in yourself. A series of 60 "Wonders" (meditations on a variety of subjects: "The Wonder of Change," "The Wonder of Attachments," etc.) will stir you in an indescribable manner. This is a bold and bright new kind of book that gently leads us on a journey of Spiritual Alchemy where the journey itself is the destination ... and the destination is our need to be spiritually whole men and women.

Most of all, you will find out through self investigation that we live in a friendly, intelligent and living universe that we can reach into and that can reach us.

**0-87542-221-7, 192 pgs., 5 1/4 x 8, softcover** $9.95

## THE SECRET OF LETTING GO
**by Guy Finley**
Whether you need to let go of a painful heartache, a destructive habit, a frightening worry or a nagging discontent, *The Secret of Letting Go* shows you how to call upon your own hidden powers and how they can take you through and beyond any challenge or problem. This book reveals the secret source of a brand-new kind of inner strength.

In the light of your new and higher self-understanding, emotional difficulties such as loneliness, fear, anxiety and frustration fade into nothingness as you happily discover they never really existed in the first place.

With a foreword by Desi Arnaz Jr., and introduction by Dr. Jesse Freeland, *The Secret of Letting Go* is a pleasing balance of questions and answers, illustrative examples, truth tales, and stimulating dialogues that allow the reader to share in the exciting discoveries that lead up to lasting self-liberation.

This is a book for the discriminating, intelligent, and sensitive reader who is looking for *real* answers.

**0-87542-223-3, 240 pgs., 5 1/4 x 8, softcover** $9.95

Prices subject to change without notice.